Routledge Revivals

The Arbitration

Gilbert Murray translated and made available to modern readers *The Epitrepontes of Menander* or *The Arbitration* for the first time in 1945. *The Arbitration* is among the most frequently quoted and most famous of Menander's plays and – being less farcical than others - belongs to his mature style. With an interesting and informative introduction, this translation will be of value to any student of Classics and Ancient Greek drama.

The Arbitration
The Epitrepontes of Menander

Translated and Completed by
Gilbert Murray

First published in 1945
by George Allen & Unwin Ltd

This edition first published in 2014 by Routledge
2 Park Square, Milton Park, Abingdon, Oxon, OX14 4RN

Simultaneously published in the USA and Canada
by Routledge
711 Third Avenue, New York, NY 10017

Routledge is an imprint of the Taylor & Francis Group, an informa business

© 1945 George Allen & Unwin Ltd

All rights reserved. No part of this book may be reprinted or reproduced or
utilised in any form or by any electronic, mechanical, or other means, now
known or hereafter invented, including photocopying and recording, or in any
information storage or retrieval system, without permission in writing from the
publishers.

Publisher's Note
The publisher has gone to great lengths to ensure the quality of this reprint but
points out that some imperfections in the original copies may be apparent.

Disclaimer
The publisher has made every effort to trace copyright holders and welcomes
correspondence from those they have been unable to contact.

A Library of Congress record exists under LC control number: 45003225

ISBN 13: 978-0-415-72994-9 (hbk)
ISBN 13: 978-1-315-85067-2 (ebk)
ISBN 13: 978-0-415-73038-9 (pbk)

THE ARBITRATION

The *Epitrepontes* of Menander

THE FRAGMENTS TRANSLATED AND
THE GAPS CONJECTURALLY
FILLED IN

BY

GILBERT MURRAY, O.M.

FORMERLY REGIUS PROFESSOR OF GREEK
IN THE UNIVERSITY OF OXFORD

London

GEORGE ALLEN & UNWIN LTD

FIRST PUBLISHED IN 1945

THE PAPER AND BINDING OF THIS
BOOK CONFORM TO THE AUTHORIZED
ECONOMY STANDARDS

Printed in Great Britain by
UNWIN BROTHERS LTD., LONDON AND WOKING

Menander, the most famous representative of the "New Comedy," was born in 342 B.C., about 140 years after Euripides, 80 years after Plato, 40 after Aristotle, a contemporary of Epicurus and Zeno the Stoic.

INTRODUCTION

THERE is great fascination in the fragments of Menander. I find it not merely in the ease and "Attic salt" of his style, or the subtle and kindly realism of his characters. There is a charm even in his conventionalities—the situations and stage tricks, now old-fashioned, which he caught at a moment when they were still young and fresh. But most of all I am attracted by his philosophy of life, ironic and yet tender, which seems to express the mind of the sensitive and highly civilized society in which he lived. It needed some fortitude in a fourth-century Athenian to keep his head and his temper in a war-ridden world where Athens' best hopes lay in ruins and men must be content, not too bitterly, to "live not as we would, but as we can."

In *The Arbitration* especially, the actual dramatic interest of the fragments preserved to us kept me wondering and trying to guess how the story was worked out, till at last I was writing the missing scenes and making up a complete play. Like the Homeric rhapsodes or "singers of stitched songs," I have "stitched" wherever possible and only invented when forced to it.

The plays are certainly actable on a modern stage. My earlier attempt, of whose faults I am more conscious now than when I made it, has been performed in several places and shown that it can amuse an audience. The present attempt is perhaps more ambitious, both because

INTRODUCTION

The Arbitration is a more serious and mature work than *The Rape of the Locks*, and because the gaps are harder to fill.

Free and natural as it is in outward appearance, there can be little doubt that the New Comedy, like all or almost all Greek drama, was in its essence the performance of a religious ritual. It took the form of what we may call a Nativity Play, celebrating the annual discovery, when all the earth seems dead, of that Renewal of Life which we think of as the New Year or the Spring, but which was to the Greeks a Being far more personal. This ritual in its simplest shape, still to be found in some Easter celebrations in Italy and Eastern Europe, used the symbol of a divine babe or lamb or young animal to typify the new life. Its birth or arrival was the gist of the celebration. At another stage, represented by Euripides' *Ion* and several fragmentary Greek tragedies, the rite has developed into drama, and the birth into a heroic myth. An outcast baby, found in the wild woods, and perhaps suckled by a mare, a cow, or some wild animal, is really the son of a god and a royal maiden and, after suitable adventures or sufferings, is duly "recognized" and accepted as the king or hero-founder of his tribe. The baby, though its presence is essential, is no longer the centre of interest. It is either allowed to relapse into the background or else its Recognition is delayed till the divine child is old enough to be a mysterious hero. Another unintended result of this dramatization is that the god is made to play a somewhat questionable

THE ARBITRATION

part. We may see him at his best in a magnificent hymn in Aeschylus' *Suppliant Women* (verses 524–600), where the heroine's sufferings form an element in a high, inscrutable purpose, and a virgin birth by the touch of the divine hand gives life to a miraculous child "perfect in blessedness"; at his worst probably in the *Ion*, where Apollo well deserves the curses which his deserted victim hurls at him in his own temple precinct. We know of no tragedies of this type after the *Ion*. It may well be that the divine ravisher was increasingly felt to be an unsuitable and indeed an impious figure. At any rate, the ritual was about this time transferred from the tragic to the comic stage, and the story brought down to a human level. In New Comedy the outcast babe is the fruit of some forbidden or secret amour, and the Recognition exalts him not to divinity but merely to wealth and fortune. The place of the god is taken, to use Aelian's contemptuous words, by "Menander's young puppies misconducting themselves at midnight festivals" (*Hist. Nat.* VII, 19).

The transference was not an entire success. Piety indeed was saved; but the more human and lifelike the general story became, the harder it was to feel much sympathy for the baby's father, who nevertheless has to be something like the hero of the play. In this play, for instance, it is hard to combine the Charisius whom we see and whom his friends describe to us with the tipsy rioter who did violence to Pamphile. His scene of repentance and bitter self-reproach—all of it, I hasten to add, the work of the real Menander—

INTRODUCTION

makes him forgivable, but still not easy to understand. We might come nearer to understanding if we listened to what Callisto had to say on the subject, or indeed if we reflected on the actual proceedings of those all-night festivals once universal throughout Europe, from ancient dances in worship of some Artemis or Dionysus to the May-day junketings of eighteenth-century England. Most, if not all, of them might have accepted as their motto the famous refrain of the *Pervigilium Veneris*:

> Cras amet qui numquam amavit, quique amavit cras amet.*

The Arbitration is among the most frequently quoted of Menander's plays. It belongs to his later style. It is less farcical than either the *Locks* or the *Samian Woman*, which is the only other play about which we have enough left to form a judgement. It has more of the smooth long speeches, in conversational style with a quiet undercurrent of wit, which were so highly appreciated in antiquity. On the other hand, the plot is richer, more romantic, and more skilfully developed; there is much deeper emotional tension. In character also, though the female parts in Menander are always good, the two earlier plays have no one comparable to Habrotonon.

As for my own work, although the extant fragments of papyrus probably cover rather more than half the play, considerably more if we count the long passages

---

* "To-morrow let him love who never has loved, and he who has loved let him love to-morrow."

THE ARBITRATION

where only two or three letters at the beginning or end of a line have been preserved, I found it much harder than in the *Locks* to conjecture the rest of the plot with any approach to confidence. I have only tried to observe Menandrian conventions and, as far as I can hope to understand it, the Menandrian spirit.

I have used chiefly the texts of Jensen and Koerte; have often consulted Mr. Frost's scholarly translation; and in matters of interpretation must express my deep obligations to the masterly treatise of Wilamowitz. On one important and doubtful problem (v. p. 123) I have accepted an attractive guess of Professor D. S. Robertson.

CHARACTERS

Charisius, *a Young Athenian*

Pamphilê, *Wife to Charisius*

Onêsimus, *Personal Servant to Charisius*

Smîcrinês, *Father to Pamphilê*

Sôphronê, *Nurse to Pamphilê*

Chaerestratus, *Next-door-Neighbour to Charisius*

Sîmias, *Older Friend to Chaerestratus*

Habrotonon, *or, for short,* Habro, *Harp-player at Chaerestratus's House*

Cârion, *Cook at Chaerestratus's House*

Syriscus, *a Charcoal-burner*

Dâvus, *a Shepherd*

Callisto, *an Arcadian nymph transformed into a Bear by Artemis*

An old Duenna in charge of Habrotonon, *Guests at House of* Chaerestratus, Syriscus's *Wife and a Baby.*

[The Scene *is the country near Athens. A tree in the foreground; the House of* Charisius *(A) back Left, that of* Chaerestratus *(B) back Right.*]

11

ACT I

Cârion, *the Cook, with* Onêsimus.

Cârion

The man who entertains this dancing girl,
Only just married, isn't he? That's odd.

Onêsimus

Yes, not so long. Five months and thirteen days.

Cârion

A daughter of old Smîcrinês, they say?
Young and attractive, eh?

Onêsimus

        Well, that depends
On taste. But yes, no doubt she has been admired,
Not only by her husband.

Cârion

        Eh? Who else?
Tell me.

Onêsimus

        I can't. I've absolutely sworn
To keep the whole thing secret.

Cârion

            Yes, quite right.
That's what I always do; swear secrecy,

THE ARBITRATION

And then, to show you know what "secret" means,
Tell them another secret of your own.
There's hardly a house I cook for, where I don't
Worm out the family troubles. For my art's sake
I must. Unless I know their state of mind
How can I give my clients what they want?
Come, out with it! I've got these innocents' dinner
All planned. I'm quite free.

ONÊSIMUS

Well, in confidence,
I don't mind telling you.

CÂRION

I'll pay you back,
Trust me, with scandals quite as rich as yours.
All knowledge comes in useful.

ONÊSIMUS

In my case
It certainly has. You see, I found it out
Two weeks back, while the master was away
At Ephesus. No one in the house but me
Knows anything. . . . Ah, there's old Sôphronê,
Her nurse.
   [*Enter* SÔPHRÔNÊ, *walking slowly.*
        She must be in it. But she can't
Do much. And we've forbidden her to hold
Any communication with her mistress.

THE ARBITRATION

[SÔPHRONÊ *stops; touches her eyes with her fingers;
then hitches her cloak up by lifting her right
arm in the air.*
Well, Sophronê, who are you looking for?

SÔPHRONÊ
The master. Has he come yet?

ONÊSIMUS
Smîcrinês?
No. You be off! You know the rule. No message.
No mischief.

SÔPHRONÊ
I am going.
[*Exit* SÔPHRONÊ.

CÂRION
What's all this?
Do you give orders?

ONÊSIMUS
I and the Young Master.
You see, as soon as ever he came back,
I asked to have a word with him alone,
And told him. Didn't he go up in smoke!
He's awfully grateful, though

CÂRION
You told him what?

THE ARBITRATION

ONÊSIMUS

It puts me in a different position
From all the others. I'm his confidant.
He's grateful to me.

CÂRION

What for?

ONÊSIMUS

Why, because

I told him.

CÂRION

Told him what?

ONÊSIMUS

Besides, I'm there
To watch; the mistress doesn't know I know.

CÂRION

You know what?

ONÊSIMUS

There's no pleasure in the world
Like knowing everything there is to know,
Especially when no one knows you know it.

CÂRION

What is it, man? What do you know?

ONÊSIMUS

I'll tell you.
[*Whispers in* CÂRION'S *ear.*

16

THE ARBITRATION

Cârion

Impossible!

Onêsimus

It's true.

Cârion

How does he take it?

Onêsimus

He's furious, and of course can't say a word.
That's the worst thing. He's got to keep it dark.

Cârion

Good God! Then that explains these harp-players
And banquets! . . . It's all frightfully upsetting
For me. I need a whole new bill of fare.
I planned a feast for lovers; just a gay,
Light-hearted, liquid, joyous, merrymaking,
And now . . . He really loved his wife, you say?

Onêsimus

He did, devotedly. Not now, of course;
No; now we act together, he and I,
We watch and punish her as she deserves.

Cârion

That's it. The man is thinking of his wife
The whole time. It's all done to punish her.
God bless me, it's a banquet of revenge,
Dark, bitter, fierce.   [*He sits down, ruminating.*

THE ARBITRATION

ONÊSIMUS
Well, what's your story?

CÂRION

Story?

ONÊSIMUS
You promised me a story as good as mine.
Man, I can't think of stories. I have duties
To think of. That's enough.

ONÊSIMUS
You promised me

A scandal.

CÂRION
Did I?—oh, well; old Telônes
Is bankrupt. Will that do?

ONÊSIMUS
Why no; I never

Heard of the man. That's no good.

CÂRION

Callicles
Is said to have a second wife in Smyrna.
I can't do more for you. I must get to work.

ONÊSIMUS
Some details, please!

THE ARBITRATION

CÂRION (*ruminating*)
        A bitter resinous sauce
With salted tunny; an old fighting cock
With mustard; no, with some Arabian spice
That burns. Oh, how my master Labdacus
Would have enjoyed this problem. I must take
Plenty of time . . . Good Lord, the guests arriving
Already!

ONÊSIMUS
    Here! You haven't paid your debt.
                        [*Exeunt into House B.*
    [*Enter from the town* SÎMIAS *and* CHAERESTRATUS.

SÎMIAS
I wish you'd think again, Chaerestratus,
Why should you lend your house, day after day,
To help Charisius to neglect his wife
And waste his substance on this dancing girl?

CHAERESTRATUS
She's not a dancing girl; she's a musician;
A good musician, too, and well behaved.
I like him, Sîmias, and I like the girl,
And if he wants my house . . . They make a noise,
Those lads, but do no harm; besides, you're there,
And you'd make any place respectable.
You know Charisius hardly looks at her.

SÎMIAS
While you do nothing else.

THE ARBITRATION

CHAERESTRATUS

He doesn't mind . . .
That's what annoys me. First, the man deserts
His own wife. So far I don't criticize.
I have no wife, and his I never met.
For all I know, she may be just the sort
No reasonable man could help deserting.
But then he goes out of his way to hire
This elegant, well-mannered harp-player,
And treats her with contempt—at any rate
With stark bad manners, hardly speaks to her . . .

SÎMIAS

Why should he? She's a slave, a hired companion.

CHAERESTRATUS

A slave, a hired . . . Oh yes. I know these girls;
They're all humbugs and liars. It's their business. . . .
Still, this one has good manners.

SÎMIAS

All the same,
Why should you let Charisius have your house
To revel in? The thing's discreditable
To both of you, and seemingly no pleasure
To anyone.

CHAERESTRATUS

Why? Well, I hardly know.
I couldn't well refuse him. Certainly
I never saw a drearier diner out.

20

THE ARBITRATION

If in his own house he was drearier still,
I only wonder why it's not his wife
Does the deserting. If she came and asked me,
I'd let the unfortunate woman have this house
To revel in till she died.

SÎMIAS

Then all the more . . .

CHAERESTRATUS

Why do I do it? Why? Because I like it.
Who wouldn't like it? It's a constant pleasure—
Free gratis, too—to see Habrotonon,
Study her movements, listen to her music,
Sometimes to talk with her. Come. In we go.

[*Exeunt into House B.*
[*Enter* CHARISIUS, *gloomy, from his own house.*
He speaks off.

CHARISIUS

Porter! I shall be out again this evening;
And if your mistress asks . . . if anyone
Who calls wishes to know where he can find me,
I am at a drinking party with some friends.
Say we expect the same young harp-player,
A very fine musician, whom we all
Greatly admire . . .

[*Enter* HABROTONON *with* DUENNA.

THE ARBITRATION

DUENNA

There, darling, you hear that!
You can't say you're neglected, when they all
Admire you so. . . . Charisius, here she is,
Fresh as a rose, and tuned like her own harp!
Come, ducky, speak to him.

HABROTONON (*stiffly*)
Good evening, Sir.

CHARISIUS (*stiffly*)
Good evening. Go in, please. You'll find them waiting,
I'll follow afterwards.
[*Exit* HABROTONON *to House B.* CHARISIUS *waits.*

DUENNA

Lovely she is, just lovely. . . . And the bill,
Twelve drachmae for to-night. (*trying it on*)
And then the night
That you forgot, five days ago.

CHARISIUS
Forgot?
Did I?

DUENNA

You did indeed, and I don't wonder.
No thought you had for anything but her.
Twice you forgot. That's three nights altogether.
Thirty-six drachmae.
[*Enter* ONÊSIMUS.

THE ARBITRATION

CHARISIUS

Here you are.

ONÊSIMUS

What's that?

[CHARISIUS *gives money and exit to House B.*
DUENNA *takes the money and puts it in her
mouth.*

DUENNA

Good-night, Sir. Blessings on you.

ONÊSIMUS

You old fraud!

Stop!

DUENNA (*with mouth full*)

There were three nights he forgot to pay.
He knows he did. He admits it.

ONÊSIMUS

Every night
You had your money. He sent me myself
To pay you, and I did. Spit out that cash!
Out with it, quick. It's no good gobbling at me.

[*Exit, pursuing* DUENNA.

PROLOGUE

[*Enter the Nymph* CALLISTO, *wearing a bearskin with
the head and jaws over her head.*

Are we alone? My mistress, Artemis,
Nowhere about? No; if she were, I'd hear
Far off the clanging of that silver bow.
No doubt she's off on the Arcadian hills,
Playing her regular part, always the same!
How well I know it all: The Huntress bright
Who roams a virgin through the virgin woods,
Fleet as the winds and free; lover of all
The young wild forest life, the kids and fawns,
And pards, and us poor bears, and everything,
And shows her love, combined with marksmanship,
By shooting us! Just like these goddesses!
No reasoning power! No common sense at all!
Nothing but charm of manner and good looks!
And such a mass of fads! To think that I
In old days believed everything she said,
Took all her ways as models to adore;
Yes, and should do so still, and still be just
As narrow, if I'd never been a bear!
    It's that that saved me. You must know me now;
Callisto, once beloved of Artemis.
Her chosen friend, and virginal as she
Until. . . . Well, really, was I much to blame?
They never think, these virgin goddesses;
It pleases them to stay eternally

THE ARBITRATION

Unloved, and then they fly into a rage
When we poor nymphs are different. If she wished
All of us Oreads to be like herself,
Why did she set us dancing, those long nights,
In ecstasy and longing, on till dawn
Through the dark woods? Others were roaming, too,
Young gods, and fauns, and satyrs, all half-drunk
With songs and moonlight. What could she expect?
She wouldn't listen. She went wild with rage,
And, seeking out some awful punishment,
Some lesson I should learn and not forget,
Transformed me on the spot, and sentenced me
To fourteen years' hard labour as a Bear.

  I did learn lessons! It's an education
Beyond the Schools, to have been a real she-bear.
I roamed the Arcadian forests, fed on fruits
And honeycomb, had fresh cubs every spring,
Suckled them, licked them into shape, and then
Forgot them and had others. I accepted
Simple things simply. All my ways became
Just what the Stoic, Zeno, recommends,
Self-serving, with no master and no slave:
I had no vain desires; I asked for no
Rare food, or costly wine; no cooks, no clothes,
No purse, no pride; and never cared at all
What other she-bears said or thought of me.
Those fourteen innocent years have taught me lessons
I've not forgotten, lessons utterly
Beyond her comprehension. She has never
Learnt anything at all. She still keeps up

25

THE ARBITRATION

The same old ways, the same old Festivals,
The same old dances by the same old moon.
She calls on all her votaries to attend
And then, of course, as anyone might guess,
Sometimes the same thing happens as with me,
And all these gods and mortals lose their wits,
And women suffer! So it has happened here.
This innocent girl herself, this Pamphilê,
Goes mad with fear. Her baby is snatched away
By that old Nurse and hidden like a crime,
From husbands, fathers, and all murderous males.
She dares not speak. Her secret shuts her off
From all she loves. She watches day by day
There, at the window, for a silent sign
The Nurse gives, passing by without a word:
"I have seen him;" "He is safe;" "In danger;" "dead."

> *[For the first sign she touches her eyes; for the second*
> *lifts her right arm; for danger, arms round*
> *waist; for dead, arms straight down.*

Alas, these humans! Always overwise
And harassed by the strange laws they devise
For their own torment; always surfeited
With fears more painful than the things they dread;
Always so eager that the strong shall wreak
For every sin due vengeance on the weak,
And most on women. If they ever knew
The truth . . . but who could show them what is true,
As now they are? The book of life that I
In my green forest read so innocently

THE ARBITRATION

And wisely, they have never understood. . . .
Poor baby, I would help it if I could.

> [*Exit* CALLISTO. *Enter from the House B* CHAERE-
> STRATUS.

> CHAERESTRATUS (*speaking off*)

All right. I have no wish to interrupt.
I'll walk about outside. I like fresh air.
And if there's any billing to be done
Or cooing, I have not the slightest wish
To bill nor yet to coo.
> [*Enter from House A* SMÎCRINÊS.

> SMÎCRINÊS (*to the Porter*)
> No, I'll not wait.

When he returns you'll tell him that I called.
The thing's past understanding. When his father
First made proposals to me, I enquired
Most carefully about him. They all told me
Charisius was a god-fearing young man,
The makings of a frugal son-in-law
And a good husband.

> CHAERESTRATUS (*aside*)
> It's old Smîcrinês,

The father-in-law. I wonder what he's heard.

> SMÎCRINÊS

I can't think what the Devil's come to him.

27

THE ARBITRATION

Dinners and drinking parties every night!
A famous cook engaged at goodness knows
What fee! And then the wine the fellow drinks!
It just amazes me. It's not so much
The intoxication; it's the awful price:
So much a spoonful! I can't understand
How any conscience can consent to it.

CHAERESTRATUS (*aside*)
I thought so. Obviously he has heard some talk.
Now he'll come raging in to stop all these
Love-feasts! It's not my business, but I think
He'll go back sorry he came.

SMÎCRINÊS
                My daughter brought him
Four talents, and he doesn't choose to be
Her housemate. He lives out. He's paying twelve
Drachmas a day to that old madam!

CHAERESTRATUS
                    Yes.
Twelve is the price. He's got his details right.

SMÎCRINÊS
Twelve for one day! Enough to keep a man
A month and six days!

THE ARBITRATION

CHAERESTRATUS

How exact! Two obols
A day; the dole that keeps a slave in gruel
And leaves him hungry!

[*Enter* SÎMIAS *from House B.*

SÎMIAS

Hi, Chaerestratus,
Your absence will be noticed.

CHAERESTRATUS

My dear man,
Do you see?

SÎMIAS

Who's that?

CHAERESTRATUS

The father of the bride.
Doesn't he scowl; like a philosopher
Gone pessimist.

SÎMIAS

No wonder. The poor man
Is worried about your harpist. He's afraid
The lawful wife indoors may find herself
Turned out and her place taken.

CHAERESTRATUS

If you'd heard him
Growling just now!

29

THE ARBITRATION

Smîcrinês

How everything combines
To thwart me! My wife dead; one daughter lost,
I did hope I could guard the livelihood
Of this one that remains.

Sîmias

How did he get
His information! I suppose some servant
Has told him things. If we could ward him off
For just a day or two we'd have a chance
To get Charisius to give up these follies
And be himself again. You'll have to help.

Chaerestratus

I can't refuse my house, but, short of that,
I'll help. I rather hate the whole affair.

Sîmias

You told me you enjoyed it.

Chaerestratus

So I do;
But somehow. . . . Well, let's put an end to it.
It's easy enough. Why shouldn't I, right now
Go up to him and tell him the whole story;
Or, better still, invite him to come in
And see things for himself. Let the old fool
Burst if he wants to.

THE ARBITRATION

SÎMIAS
Silence on your life!
That would wreck everything beyond repair.
Don't talk so.

SMÎCRINÊS (*rising*)
I'll go home.

CHAERESTRATUS
Yes, do, by all means:
Or, better still, to the Devil.

SMÎCRINÊS
I'll go home,
I want first to make certain of the facts
About my daughter's treatment; then I'll think
Calmly what line to take about the man.
[*Exit*

SÎMIAS
Ought we to warn Charisius that he's here?

CHAERESTRATUS
Yes, rather. What an old pest! That's the way
To break a household up.

SÎMIAS
I only wish
He'd break up others. [*Singing heard off*

CHAERESTRATUS
Others?

31

THE ARBITRATION

SÎMIAS

And begin

By one next door.

CHAERESTRATUS

Do you mean mine?

SÎMIAS

Yes, my friend,

Yours. But meantime let's warn Charisius.

CHAERESTRATUS

Mine? ...

But let's go in. I see a noisy crowd
Making this way, young lads and not too sober.
It's better not to meet them.

SÎMIAS

Can you help it?

Unhappy man, these are our fellow-guests!

[*Exeunt into House.*

CHORUS OF REVELLERS

I long to be a loony,
A laughing, leaping loony;
As mad as all those others
Renowned in tragic story,
Who run so wild and moony
On murdering their mothers.
I don't know which the best is,
Alcmaeon or Orestes;

32

THE ARBITRATION

They both get rather gory
When murdering their mothers.
    I don't want all the bother
Of murdering my mother.
I don't want blood and slaughter;
Red wine is what I'm after;
It's wine I want and laughter.
With no allaying water.
    Oh, when the night is moony,
And springtime soft and spoony,
It's then I'll be a loony,
With no allaying water,
A laughing, leaping loony
With no allaying water!
                    [*They straggle into the House.*

ACT II

Onêsimus *alone*.

Onêsimus

A slippery business, all the life of man!
Take me, now. All my duties summed together,
My fatherland, my refuge and my law,
My judge of every right and every wrong,
Is just my master. And, God only knows
How slippery *he* is! Still, we stand together,
We two. We're partners now in my discovery.
As soon as he got back from Ephesus,
I went straight up, took him aside, and told him
So naturally he's grateful—Naturally,
He must be grateful. . . . This old man, of course,
Annoys us and will soon annoy us more.
No doubt his daughter's told him half the story,
Young Habro and the cook and the rare wines,
And what they all cost, and lots more as well.
I don't suppose she said one word about
Her own affair, which started all the trouble.
All right, it's up to me. If the old man
Knew everything, of course he'd take our side,
But can we tell him? Obviously we can't,
A husband can't proclaim his own dishonour.
Impossible! . . . Well, since I'm not allowed
To let the man know what he doesn't know,
I've got to make him un-know what he knows.
That's a bit puzzling.

34

THE ARBITRATION

[*Enter* SMÎCRINÊS *from House A.*
Oh, good morning, Sir.

SMÎCRINÊS

Look here, rogue; are you honest?

ONÊSIMUS

That is hardly
For me to say, Sir. You might ask my master.

SMÎCRINÊS

I'd sooner ask your mistress. I've just come
From talking to her, and I have some questions
To put to you.

ONÊSIMUS

Ah, yes, Sir! These young wives;
They're sensitive. They do exaggerate,
Their feelings are so strong. You can't believe
All that a young wife says.

SMÎCRINÊS

Ah, that's so, is it?
They lie like troopers to defend their husbands?
I thought as much. No, come; tell me the truth,
I've heard unpleasant stories in the town . . .

ONÊSIMUS

About our mistress?

THE ARBITRATION

SMÎCRINÊS

No, you fool, about

Your master.

ONÊSIMUS

Oh, I'm glad, Sir. Then there's nothing
To worry about. Of course you need not heed them,
People in Athens would say anything,
Just for the pleasure of inventing.

SMÎCRINÊS

Ah;

That's what *she* says.

ONÊSIMUS

She does? (*To himself.*) Good

business! Yes,
Of course she does!—I heard some talk myself
About these parties the young man next door
Is giving.

SMÎCRINÊS

What? It's not my son-in-law

Who gives them?

ONÊSIMUS

Oh, no, no! Of course it's young

Chaerestratus, who lives there. He's unmarried
And rich, and, I'm afraid, Sir, not quite wise.
He's lost his head over a pretty girl
Who plays the harp.

SMÎCRINÊS

They say my son-in-law

Is always there?

36

THE ARBITRATION

ONÊSIMUS

Why, yes, Sir; pretty often.
He felt . . . we both felt . . . we could be some use
To his young friends by keeping things decorous,
And seeing he's not cheated. He's so helpless.

SMÎCRINÊS

Keep them decorous, does he? Doesn't he
Stay out all night? The porter said. . . .

ONÊSIMUS

Oh, no, Sir!
When he's been late, I've let him in myself.
He's not the man to enjoy that kind of thing.

SMÎCRINÊS

Now, once for all, who is it pays the bills?
Is it my son-in-law?

ONÊSIMUS

What an idea!
My master!—Oh, I see how that's got round.
Quite often it's arranged that I myself
Should overlook the bills, to see our host
Is not being cheated. Some one must have seen me,
And thought, of course, it was my master's money.

THE ARBITRATION

SMÎCRINÊS

Thanks, my good fellow. You're an honest man.
You've taken a great burden off my mind.
I'll tell my daughter I did wrong to doubt her.

[*Exit to House.*

ONÊSIMUS

How easy lying is! And how convenient!
And think what trouble people give themselves
Telling the truth! To know it and not tell it
Is my plan—Well, we've got young Pamphilê
Fixed. If she tells of us we tell of her.
I'll go and let the master know he's safe.

[*Exit, as* DÂVUS *and* SYRISCUS, *followed by* SYRIS-
CUS'S WIFE *carrying a baby, enter. As* ONÊ-
SIMUS *goes off,* SYRISCUS *catches at him.*

SYRISCUS

Here! Wait a moment.

ONÊSIMUS
No. I'm busy.

[*Exit.*

DÂVUS (*to* SYRISCUS)
Stop!

SYRISCUS

You won't face justice!

DÂVUS
You're blackmailing me,
Confound you! . . . You can't have what isn't yours.

38

THE ARBITRATION

SYRISCUS

We need an arbitrator.

DÂVUS

Oh, all right.

For God's sake find one.

SYRISCUS

Who do you think would do?

DÂVUS

I don't mind. Anyone . . . It serves me right.
Why did I give him anything?

SYRISCUS

Look there.

[SMÎCRINÊS *comes out of the House.*

Will that man do?

DÂVUS

All right.

SYRISCUS

Excuse me, Sir,
But might I ask you, if you'd be so kind,
To spare us a few moments of your time?

SMÎCRINÊS

You? What about?

SYRISCUS

We are having a dispute,

A matter of business.

THE ARBITRATION

SMÎCRINÊS
Well, what's that to me?

SYRISCUS
We want an honest judge to arbitrate
Between us. If there's nothing to prevent you,
Do be our judge.

SMÎCRINÊS
You'll come to a bad end,
You two; rascals in goatskins walking round
And arguing points of law!

SYRISCUS
Yes, Sir, but still . . .
The thing's quite short and easy to explain.
Please, father, as a kindness! In God's name
[*In a rhetorical manner.*
I beg you, don't reject us. At all times
And in all regions Justice should prevail,
And, in the common interest of mankind,
'Tis the concern of all who pass to see
Justice upheld.

DÂVUS (*to himself*)
Not half an orator,
This chap I've got mixed up with! Why on earth
Did I go shares?

SMÎCRINÊS
You promise to accept
My judgement?

40

THE ARBITRATION

SYRISCUS
Yes, whatever it may be.

SMÎCRINÊS
All right, I'll hear the case. Why shouldn't I?
Come, you who've not said anything, begin.

DÂVUS
I'll start a bit back, just to make things clear,
Before he came in. I was with my sheep
Alone, up in the wood beyond those farms.
About a month ago it was; I found
A baby laid out with a necklace on him
And stuff like this.

SYRISCUS
That's what it's all about.

DÂVUS
He says you're not to speak!

SMÎCRINÊS
You'll have my stick
About you if you talk before your turn.

DÂVUS
And quite right too!

SMÎCRINÊS
Go on.

41

THE ARBITRATION

Dâvus

I'm going on.
I picked it up and took it home to rear
As mine. At least, that's what I meant at first;
Then, in the night came second thoughts, the kind
That always come at night. "Why should I take
To nursing babies? How can I afford it?
Do I really want more worries than I've got?"
Well, that's how I was feeling when, at dawn,
Again I took the sheep out, and this man
Came to the same place . . . he's a charcoal-burner . . .
To saw some stumps. I'd known him well before.
We fell to talking and he saw that I
Was in bad spirits. "Why so glum," he said,
"What's wrong, mate?" Well, I couldn't hold my
    tongue!
I told him the whole business, how I'd found
The baby and picked it up; and, straight away,
Before I'd finished speaking, he began
Begging me, breaking it at every point,
"Oh, Dâvus, as you hope for any luck,
"Give me that baby. Do! Fortune will bless you,
"And set you free! I have a wife," he said,
"Who had a baby, and it died." He meant
That woman there, who's carrying the baby.

Smîcrinês

You begged him, you?

Syriscus

I did, Sir,

42

THE ARBITRATION

DÂVUS

>The whole day
He kept on worrying at me, till at last
I agreed and gave it, and he went away
Showering his blessings on me. Why, he took
And kissed my hands!

SMÎCRINÊS
You kissed his hands?

SYRISCUS

>I did.

DÂVUS
So off he went; and now he suddenly
Comes at me, with his wife, and makes a claim
To all the stuff . . . just odds and ends, no value . . .
I found there with the baby, and complains
Because I keep it and won't give it him.
I say he should be thankful that he's got,
Out of my find, the share he asked me for.
He has no right to come cross-questioning me
Whether I gave him everything I found.
Suppose he'd been there and we'd found the things
Together, why, we'd only have gone halves;
Each would have had his share. . . . And now, good
> Lord,
When you weren't there and I found everything
That was found, you must have the lot, and I
Nothing at all!

THE ARBITRATION

There's only one thing more,
I gave you something that was mine to give;
Well, if you like it, keep it; if you don't,
Or if you've changed your mind, then give it back.
That isn't cheating me nor yet yourself.
But first to accept my gift with thanks, and then
Come bullying to take everything I've got,
It can't be done. That's all I have to say.

SYRISCUS

He's finished?

SMÎCRINÊS
Yes, you heard. He's finished.

SYRISCUS

Good.

I follow on. He and he only found
The baby. What he says is quite correct.
That's how it happened, father. I deny
Nothing. I begged and prayed him for the child,
And got it. All quite true. But then a shepherd,
One of his mates, to whom he'd talked about it,
Brought me the news that with the child he'd found
Some ornaments. To claim those ornaments
Here comes the owner. . . . Pass the baby, wife . . .
This person, Dâvus, asks you for his clothes,
Necklets and tokens of identity.
They were put out, he says, for him to wear,
And not for you to swallow. That's his claim,
And I, his legal representative . . .

44

THE ARBITRATION

You made me so by giving him to me . . .
Endorse that claim. That is the point, your Honour.
And, as I see it, all you have to do
Is to pronounce due judgement about these
Gold trinkets or whatever else they are;
Should they be kept, according to the gift
Of the unknown mother, till the child can use them,
Or handed to this robber of the child,
As being first finder of what isn't his?
Do you ask me why I didn't claim the things
The first day, when I asked him for the baby?
Because I had no right to speak for him
At that time. I've not come to claim the things
Now for myself. No "going halves" for me;
No "finding's keeping." If your finding leaves
An innocent person wronged, I call it theft.
Besides, Sir, think: this child may prove to be
Of higher birth than ours. If he's brought up
Among day-labourers, won't he think their ways
Common and fly to his own natural bent:
Seek some high-class adventure, carry arms,
Hunt lions or run races in the Games?
You've often seen the tragedies, I'm sure;
You know the sort of thing. One . . . Neleus, was it?
And Pelias . . . you remember? . . . They were found
By an old goatherd, in a goatskin, just
Like mine; and when he saw they were his betters
He told them all the story, how he found them
And took them in; then he produced a bag
All crammed with tokens of identity,

45

THE ARBITRATION

Which taught them the whole truth about themselves
And turned the one-time goatherds into kings.
Had Dâvus found that bag, why he'd have sold
The tokens in the hope of making, say,
Some dozen drachmas, and those splendid princes
Would, all their lives, have not known who they were!
It can't be right that I should have the baby
To rear and feed, while Dâvus grabs the tokens,
The sole clue to its future, and destroys them.
By tokens before now men have been saved
From marrying their sisters; men have found
Their mothers in distress and rescued them;
One woman saved her brother—all through tokens!
And life is full of pitfalls, which a man
Can only avoid by looking far ahead
And using all the clues available.
"If you don't like it, give it back," he says,
And counts that a strong point. No. Quite unfair!
We prove you're bound in justice to disgorge
The baby's clues, and you reply by claiming
To take the baby himself, and so be free
To play the rogue with everything of his
That chance may have preserved. There. That's my
    case.
Give judgement, Sir, as you consider just.

SMÎCRINÊS

That's easy. Everything that was laid out
Beside the baby is the baby's own.
That's my decision.

THE ARBITRATION

DÂVUS

Good; and what about
The baby itself?

SMÎCRINÊS

By Zeus, I can't award
The baby to the man who is trying to rob it.
The baby must be his who brought it help
And stopped you when you meant to do it wrong.

SYRISCUS

God bless you, Sir!

DÂVUS

No, damn it! That's too bad!
Too bad, by Zeus the Saviour! I who found
Everything, must be stripped of everything?
My whole find going to the fool who found
Nothing! You mean, I've got to give them up?

SMÎCRINÊS

That's my decision.

DÂVUS

It's a shocking judgement.
Plague take me, it's a scandal!

SMÎCRINÊS

Come, be quick.

DÂVUS

Lord Zeus, what treatment!

47

THE ARBITRATION

SYRISCUS

    Here, let's see the things.
Untie that bag. I know that's where you keep them . . .
Please, wait a bit, Sir, till he gives them up.

DÂVUS

Why did I ever trust this man to judge?

SMÎCRINÊS

Quick, jailbird! Hand them over.

DÂVUS

     It's a scandal!
A scandal! (*He hands over the wallet.*)

SMÎCRINÊS

Got them all?

SYRISCUS

    I think I have,
Unless he swallowed some of them while I
Was pleading, and he knew that he was caught.

DÂVUS

I couldn't have believed it!

SYRISCUS

    Thank you, Sir.
Good-bye. I wish all judges were like you.
       [*Exit* SMÎCRINÊS.

THE ARBITRATION

DÂVUS

The unfairness of it all! By Hercules,
I never heard of such a shocking judgement.

SYRISCUS

You tried to cheat.

DÂVUS

Oh, you impostor, you!
You'll keep them for the baby, I don't think!
I'll watch you night and day.

SYRISCUS

Oh, take a walk!
Amuse yourself!

[*Exit* DÂVUS.
Now, wife, pick up these trinkets
And take them in to the master. We'll stay here
To-night; then home, after the rents are paid,
To-morrow. First, though, for a proper list.
You've got a box? No box? Well, fold your dress
To hold them. (SYRISCUS *and his* WIFE *sit down and
examine the tokens.*)
[*Enter from House B* ONÊSIMUS.

ONÊSIMUS

Never was a slower cook
Seen in this world! By this time yesterday
They were half through dessert.

49

D

THE ARBITRATION

SYRISCUS

This seems to be
A sort of cock, a stout one. Take it, wife.
A gold thing set with stones. A double axe.

ONÊSIMUS

Hello, what's this? (*Comes and looks over* SYRISCUS's
shoulder.)

SYRISCUS

A queer gold-plated ring,
Gold upon iron. The seal a bull or goat,
I can't say which. But here's the artist's name;
Kleostratus, the inscription says.

ONÊSIMUS

Let's look!
[ONÊSIMUS *seizes the ring.*

SYRISCUS

Humph! Who the devil . . .

ONÊSIMUS

It is!

SYRISCUS

What is?

ONÊSIMUS

This ring.

It's it!

THE ARBITRATION

SYRISCUS

It's what? I don't know what you mean.

ONÊSIMUS

This is Charisius's, my master's ring.

SYRISCUS

You're cracked.

ONÊSIMUS

The one he lost.

SYRISCUS

Put down that ring,

Confound you!

ONÊSIMUS

Let you keep our ring? I like that.
Where did you get it from?

SYRISCUS

By all the gods,
This is too bad! That's what it is to try
To save the treasures of an orphan child.
Everyone's first thought is to grab at them.
Put down that ring, I tell you.

ONÊSIMUS

Are you joking?
I swear by all the gods, this is my master's.

THE ARBITRATION

SYRISCUS

I'd sooner have my throat cut, any day
Than let this man . . . All right. My mind's made up.
I'll go to law with all the thieves in Greece,
One after the other. It's the baby's stuff,
Not mine . . . A golden twist. Here, take it, wife.
Some torn red silk. Yes; take them all inside.

[*Exit* WIFE *to House B.*

Now what have you to say to me?

ONÊSIMUS

To say?
This ring's Charisius's. It's this, he told me,
He lost once on a spree.

SYRISCUS

Oh, well, I serve
His friend next door. So keep it if you like,
Yourself, or let me have it to produce
When wanted.

ONÊSIMUS

H'm. I'd like to keep the thing.

SYRISCUS

It's all the same to me. I think we're bound
For the same house here, aren't we?

52

THE ARBITRATION

Onêsimus

Yes; but now
They're having company. It mightn't be
Quite tactful to reveal all this just now
To the young master. Will to-morrow do?

Syriscus

To'morrow'll do. I'm ready to submit
The whole dispute to any judge you like,
One speech each side. I've not done badly that way
Already. No more charcoal stumps for me!
I'll take to law suits. It's the only way
For honest men to live their lives to-day.

[*Exeunt both into House B.*

ACT III

Onêsimus *alone.*

That ring! I've started off five times or more
To show it to the Master. Then somehow
When I've come up and got him to myself,
I daren't . . . I sometimes doubt if it was wise
To tell him the other thing. "God damn the rogue
Who told me!" is what he mutters to himself
When he's alone. I've heard him. Yes, quite often
He says that . . . H'm, suppose he made it up
With her? Well, that would be the end of me!
To have told her secret, fatal! Bad enough
Even to have known it. . . . Yes, I am sure it's best
To make no further trouble. Why, even now
We're in for a quite fairly devilish row.

> [*Enter* Habrotonon *from the House of* Chaere-
> stratus.

Habrotonon (*speaking off*)
Excuse me, gentlemen! . . . I beg you, Sir,
You only cause me annoyance . . . Well, if ever
A helpless girl was made a laughing stock!
They said the man had fallen in love with me;
It's not love, it's repulsion; something quite
Inhuman! He won't even let me sit
At the same table. I must keep far off!

54

THE ARBITRATION

ONÊSIMUS (*musing over the ring*)
Return it to the man I got it from?
That's hardly sensible.

HABROTONON
The wretched man,
What is he wasting all that money for?
For all he has got from me, I'm qualified
To carry the holy basket to the Goddess,
Lord save us! "Free from contact with a male
For three days."

ONÊSIMUS
What on earth am I to do?
I ask you; what on earth?
[*Enter* SYRISCUS *from the House of* CHARISIUS.
HABROTONON *begins to take notice.*

SYRISCUS
Where can he be?
I've hunted for him everywhere inside (*seeing* ONÊSIMUS).
Hullo! Look here, mate. Either give me back
That ring or show it to the man you mean
To show it to. Let's get the business settled.
I can't wait longer.

ONÊSIMUS
See, man; it's like this.
It really does belong . . . so much I know
For certain . . . to Charisius. But I somehow
Don't like to show it him. It's much the same
As telling him he's the father of that baby
The ring was found with.

55

THE ARBITRATION

SYRISCUS

How do you mean, you fool?

ONÊSIMUS

He lost it last year at the Tauropolia;
So much we know. There was an all-night dance,
Women as well as men. One can but think
He gave it as a present to some girl
He got mixed up with. I suppose it's she
Who had this baby and left it in the wood.
If one could find the girl, and then produce
This ring, it would be clinching; but not now.
To show it now would only make suspicion
And trouble.

SYRISCUS

It's your business, anyhow,
Not mine. But if you're trying to put me off,
Or if you expect to make me pay you something
To get it back, you make a great mistake.
I don't go halves in anything!

ONÊSIMUS

All right.

Who asked you to?

SYRISCUS

I've got a job in town
Just now, but when it's finished, I'll come back
And see what's to be done.

[*Exit* SYRISCUS.

THE ARBITRATION

HABROTONON

Onêsimus,
Is it the child the woman there indoors
Is nursing, that this charcoal-burner found?

ONÊSIMUS

Yes, so he says.

HABROTONON

It's such a pretty creature!
Poor child!

ONÊSIMUS

And lying beside it was this ring,
My master's.

HABROTONON

What an awful thing! Just think!
That baby is your master's son, your own
Young master. You can't mean to leave him there
In slavery! You could be hanged for that.

ONÊSIMUS

I don't know what to do. I've just explained,
Nobody knows the mother.

HABROTONON

And you say
He lost the ring at last year's Tauropolia?

ONÊSIMUS

They'd all of them been drinking, so the boy
Said who attended him.

57

THE ARBITRATION

HABROTONON
He must have wandered
Away alone, and fallen upon some girl
Fresh from the women's midnight dance—Why, once
A thing like that happened when I was there.

ONÊSIMUS
When you were there?

HABROTONON
Yes, that was last year, too.
I had come to play the harp at what they call
The Younger Girls' dance, and this girl was there
Among them, laughing. I could join their play
Myself then. At that time I didn't know
What a man was.

ONÊSIMUS (*ironically*)
Says you!

HABROTONON (*indignant*)
By Aphrodite,
I swear!

ONÊSIMUS
This girl, you don't know who she was?

HABROTONON
I could find out. I know she was a friend
Of some one in my party.

THE ARBITRATION

ONÊSIMUS
Did you hear
Her father's name?

HABROTONON
No, I know nothing more.
I am sure I'd know her if we met again.
My goodness, she was pretty! And, they said,
From a rich house.

ONÊSIMUS
Most likely it's the same.

HABROTONON
I don't know. She was with us, but strayed off.
Then later, all of a sudden, back she came
Running, in tears, tearing her hair. She'd spoilt
A lovely mantle, soft Tarentine silk;
It was all tatters.

ONÊSIMUS
Did she have this ring?

HABROTONON
She may have had. She didn't show it me.
I won't invent things.

ONÊSIMUS
What am I to do?

59

THE ARBITRATION

HABROTONON

That's your look-out . . . But if you're sensible,
And ask for my advice, you'll go and show him
His ring. Suppose that girl was a free maiden.
He can't be left not knowing what he's done.

ONÊSIMUS

First, let us find out who the woman was.
There, Habro, that's a job for you and me
Together.

HABROTONON

No, I couldn't; not until
I really know for certain who the man was
Who wronged her. I should be afraid to go
And tell those ladies I was with a story
That might be false. That ring may well have been
A pledge that one of his companions took,
And then lost. Or he may have been at dice
And put the ring up as a stake; or perhaps
He owed some debt and had no cash, and so
Paid with the ring. Hundreds of things like that
Happen at drinking bouts. Until I know
The man who wronged her I don't want to seek
That girl out or spread any kind of gossip
To anyone.

ONÊSIMUS

No; I'm afraid you're right.
Then, what the Devil . . .

60

THE ARBITRATION

HABROTONON
                    Look, Onêsimus.
What do you say to this? The thought has just
Struck me. Suppose . . . suppose I make the whole
Adventure mine. I'll take the ring and go
In there to play to them.

ONÊSIMUS
                    Go on. Explain.
Though I can guess.

HABROTONON
                    He'll see it on my finger.
He'll ask me where I got it; and I'll say,
"At last year's Tauropolia, when I was
An innocent girl." All that that other girl
Went through I'll tell as happening to myself . . .
I know it well enough!

ONÊSIMUS
                    Magnificent!

HABROTONON
Then, if it strikes a chord in him, he'll come
Bursting to question me . . . He's tipsy, too;
He'll blurt out the whole story without waiting
For me to speak. I'll just say "Yes" to all
He says, and never risk making mistakes
By speaking first.

THE ARBITRATION

Onêsimus
Oh, good! Better than good!

Habrotonon
I'll hang my head and all that, and just murmur
The obvious things. It's safe enough. "How cruel
You were to me! A cave-man!"

Onêsimus
Capital!

Habrotonon
And "Oh, how violently you threw me down!"
And "That poor cloak I ruined"! That's the kind
Of talk. But first of all I'll go indoors
And get the baby, and drop a tear, and kiss it,
And ask the woman where she got it.

Onêsimus
Glory!

Habrotonon
And bring it in; and then the final stroke;
"So now you are a father!" and I show him
The foundling.

Onêsimus
Oh, Habrotonon, what cheek!
What devilry!

THE ARBITRATION

HABROTONON

If once we have the proof,
And know that he's the father, then we'll make
Inquiries at our ease to find the mother.

ONÊSIMUS (*suspiciously*)

There's one thing you've not mentioned. You'll be
     given
Your freedom. If he once believes that you're
The mother of his child he'll have you freed.

HABROTONON (*musing*)

I don't know. Oh, I wonder!

ONÊSIMUS

                    You don't know?
Don't you? Look here, do I get any good
From all this?

HABROTONON

         Yes, by the Two Goddesses!
However it ends, I owe it all to you.

ONÊSIMUS

Ah, but suppose, when once you've caught your man,
You leave things, and forget about the true
Mother; that leaves me planted.

THE ARBITRATION

Habrotonon
                    Why should I
Do that? Do you think I'm pining for a baby?
If only I could be free! Oh, God in heaven,
After all this, that's the reward I pray for!

Onêsimus
I hope you get it.

Habrotonon
You accept my plan?

Onêsimus
With all my heart. And if you do try on
Some funny business, there'll be time enough
To fight you. Trust me, I'll know what to do.
Just for the present, though, I'll wait and see.

Habrotonon
You do agree, then?

Onêsimus
I agree.

Habrotonon
                    Then quick,
Give me the ring.

Onêsimus
There!

THE ARBITRATION

HABROTONON

> Thanks. O blessed Goddess,
Persuasion, hear me! Teach me how to tell
My story right, and may the end be well!

> [*Exit* HABROTONON.

ONÊSIMUS

By Jove, she has initiative, that girl!
She finds there isn't any road to freedom
Through love; that's a blind alley; so she turns
The opposite way. . . . Yes, I suppose I'll always
Remain a slave. A moonstruck, drivelling ass!
Can't think ahead! . . . Of course, if she has luck
I might get something. . . . That'd be only fair . . .
Fair? What a calculation, to expect
Fair dealing from a woman! You poor fool!
I only hope there's no new trouble brewing . . .
The mistress, too. She's in a slippery place.
They may find, any time, some free man's daughter
Was mother to that baby. If they do,
He'll marry her in a twinkling, and dismiss
Our Pamphilê to her father. In that case,
I'm nicely saved out of the wrath to come . . .
Well, I've kept clear this time! And after this
I abjure all meddling. Catch me ever again
Poking my nose in other folks' affairs,
Or telling tales—I give you leave to cut
My tonsils out! . . . But who's this coming up?
Oh, Smîcrinês again; back from the city;
And showing signs of mental perturbation! (*amused*)
I shouldn't wonder if he'd heard some news

THE ARBITRATION

Not fully in accord with what I told him.
I'd better vanish quietly and pretend
Not to have seen him. Yes, and first find out
For certain what young Habro's been about.
> [*Exit* Onêsimus *as* Smîcrinês *enters.*

SMÎCRINÊS

I hate this gossip. I believe they want
To make a fool of me. "Never at home;
Drunken; extravagant;" I don't believe it.
The city is humming with that sort of scandal.
Well, this time I'm determined to find out
The actual truth of the matter. For three nights
They said, he hasn't slept at home; he's drinking,
And bringing open shame upon his parents
With some disreputable harpist girl.
And yet that honest fellow I talked with here
Assured me that he had really lived at home
These last three days, and any previous trouble
He had had with Pamphilê had quite blown over.
He struck me as truthful. Pest! How can I tell
Which to believe? I didn't like those people
In Athens. They enjoyed tormenting me,
Knowing I hate extravagance. They grinned
Into my face and rattled off this story
Of special cooks and feasts and dancing girls
And dice and noise and laughter. Very likely
They made it all up, just to worry me.
If so, well, I won't let it. After all
That servant knew the facts. One man who knows

THE ARBITRATION

Is worth a hundred gossips. And besides
I have another witness, who knows all
And cares for me, and for my property,
And her own happiness. My daughter says
All's well. I must believe my only child.
> [*Guests burst tumultuously out of* CHAERESTRATUS'S
> *House.*

But what's all this? The party breaking up?
I warned Charisius not to get mixed up
With people of that sort. That man next door's
Impossible. How could he ever hope
To keep him straight?

CÂRION (*off*)
>   I won't be just turned out
Like this, Sir! You're insulting my profession.
> [*Enter* CÂRION, *pushed out by* SÎMIAS.

SÎMIAS
Go, go. The party's finished.

CÂRION
>   What? Before
They've tasted my best sauce? It isn't decent.
You'll never get another cook to make
Such sauces—all this fuss about a baby!

SMÎCRINÊS
Quite a *recherché* feast that man next door
Is giving!

THE ARBITRATION

CÂRION

Insult upon insult! No;
I won't endure it. Off they slink and leave
Their food untouched. I swear if ever again
They give a feast and one of them comes begging
For a good cook . . . well, they can go to Heaven
And get one!

SMÎCRINÊS

Tell me, Cook; what's happening here?

CÂRION

What's happening? Why they're making me a jest
In Athens, all because that stupid girl
Breaks in with, first, her ring and, next, her baby,
And upsets everyone, and vows it's his.
And he's struck dumb and has acknowledged it,
And no one knows which way to look; and so
They're all gone, leaving me a laughing-stock.

SMÎCRINÊS

All gone?

CÂRION

Charisius and the harping girl
Are there alone, and that infernal baby.

SMÎCRINÊS

Charisius? Why's he there?

THE ARBITRATION

CÂRION

The party's spoilt,
And when a party's spoilt the whole town thinks
The cook's to blame.

SMÎCRINÊS

But why Charisius? Why
Charisius?

CÂRION

First, they said I took too long
Preparing. Every self-respecting Cook
Needs time.

SMÎCRINÊS

You said Charisius. You must mean
The host, Chaerestratus.

CÂRION

Of course I mean
The host, the father of this wretched baby;
His name's Charisius, and that's his house,
Next door. Then, secondly, they laid my things
In the wrong order . . .

SMÎCRINÊS

Oh, get out! Get out!

CÂRION

What? I protest.

[SMÎCRINÊS *drives* CÂRION *out.*

THE ARBITRATION

SMÎCRINÊS

Then those who lied to me
Were my own household! The loud streets and gutters
Spoke the bare truth, and not quite all the truth.
Damnation! . . . But this simplifies the case.
I'll send my agent to insist at once
That he restores my daughter and her dowry.
She's still quite young. I'll find her a good husband
In spite of them. This daughter I can save.

[*Enter* CHAERESTRATUS *and* SÎMIAS.

CHAERESTRATUS

O Hercules, enough! Where's Sîmias?
Let's get away at once. . . . By Helios, yes,
I liked that girl, and I don't understand
Charisius. I don't like it.

SÎMIAS

Nor do I.
I always told you so.

SMÎCRINÊS

Thank God my daughter
Is childless! How much harder it would be
To take her back if she had borne that man
A child . . . (*going up to them*) Excuse me, Sirs, I think
    you both
Were dining with Charisius. Is it true
This friend of yours gave here, day after day,
A series of continuous drinking-bouts
In a hired house? He was ashamed, I hear,

70

THE ARBITRATION

To show his face at home, but not ashamed
To breed a bastard from a prostitute . . .

CHAERESTRATUS

No, you're in error, Sir. This house is mine.
The mother of that child is a musician
Of charm and talent. If your son-in-law
Displeases you, no doubt you have every right
To take your daughter home and break the marriage,
But that's no reason to come meddling here
Using strong language . . .

SÎMIAS

Hush! (*to* SMÎCRINÊS) I

think you wrong
Charisius. I know nothing of this amour
He seems to have had, but I'm quite sure it's finished.
His manner to this girl . . . we all have noticed . . .
Is most reserved. He's an unhappy man,
Of that I'm sure. I beg you to think well
Before you add to his unhappiness.

SMÎCRINÊS

Think about *him*? Why, wouldn't that be meddling
And interfering, just the things your friend
Objects to? He would sooner I went home
Taking my daughter with me? Very good.
That's what I've come to do; that's why I summon
You two men, in accordance with the law,
To bear true witness how Charisius lives,

THE ARBITRATION

And how he has clearly shown himself unworthy
To be my daughter's husband. Is that clear?

Sîmias

I beg, before you ask us, Smîcrinês,
You'll make quite sure it's what you really wish.
I have known Charisius many years. I know
His nature, and am sure that these last days
Something has made him mad, unlike himself.
Speak to him as a father. All the shame
You heap upon Charisius will spring back
And strike your innocent daughter.

Smîcrinês

                                     These last days!
When did he get this harping girl with child?
What was his nature then? It's not my nature
To leave my daughter wedded to a rake
Who wastes her dowry on his harping girls
And cooks.

Sîmias

                    I tell you he is not like that.
He simply hates the sort of thing men call
A life of pleasure; "Drunk with so-and-so";
"Fifty gold Darics on a single feast . . ."
"This girl to-night and that to-morrow." No,
It's not his style. He has a natural pride,
I know, which makes him feel that sort of life
Disgusting.

THE ARBITRATION

SMÎCRINÊS

He has deceived you, as he once
Did me. But not again; no, not again
Or call me no Athenian! What, that man
My son-in-law? Him and his natural pride!
I hope it chokes him. What does he expect?
To live upon her dowry, and spend his days
Drunk in the tavern where he found that slut,
And live with her, thinking that we don't know,
And take his little bastard for his heir . . .

SÎMIAS

Good-bye, Sir. That's enough.

> [*Exit* SÎMIAS *and* CHAERESTRATUS.

SMÎCRINÊS

I must be calm.
It's strange how they defend him. It may be
He once was honest. It must be that woman,
That harping harlot, has corrupted him,
She and her brat . . . I'll have her whipped from Athens!

> [*Enter* SYRISCUS.

SYRISCUS

It's rather a delicate business; here's my wife,
Insists that I must see that harper girl
And find if Dâvus really gave us all
The trinkets. . . . Ah, that kind old gentleman
Who helped me so! I'm sure he'd introduce me . . .
Allow me to congratulate you, Sir;

73

THE ARBITRATION

True happiness is to make others happy,
And that you have done indeed. It's all your work;
That poor lost baby saved, the father found
Both re-united to the lovely mother,
All thanks to you!

SMÎCRINÊS

Infernal impudence!
Who sent you here to mock me? Out, you dog!

SYRISCUS

Help! Help! What have I done? This is a case
For arbitration—peaceful arbitration . . .
[*Exit* SMÎCRINÊS, *driving* SYRISCUS *before him.*

ACT IV

SMÎCRINÊS *and* PAMPHILÊ *come out of* CHARISIUS'S
House, talking.

SMÎCRINÊS
For you, my child, I am making the whole business
As easy as possible. You take no part
In the discussion; you make no complaint,
No charges. Nobody need hear a word
Of his own wasteful conduct or the wrongs
He has done to *you*. All that I don't discuss.
My case is amply strong enough without it.
"I gave my daughter to this man believing
He was a man of substance; now I find
He is not in a position to support her,
And take her back. Who wouldn't?"—As for you,
My dear, don't be afraid that you'll be left
Stranded. I know a man of good position,
A friend to me, steady and well-connected,
Who'll marry you at once.

PAMPHILÊ
            Oh, father, stop!
Please—though I feel it's really you, not I,
Who ought to say all this. You are so much wiser
Than I, and put things better. But this time
I think it's I who see what's right and true.
If he's committed some great public crime,
That's for the law to deal with, not for me.

THE ARBITRATION

But if it's only something personal
To me, it's odd that I've not noticed it.
I don't know what it is. No doubt I'm stupid;
A woman seldom has the brains to judge
Of public things, but surely in her own
Sphere, where she's touched herself, she is fairly sharp.
I don't feel wronged; but if you think I am,
Please tell me what he has done! I only know
The old accepted law for man and wife;
That, all life long, he should be kind to her,
And she, all life long, do what pleases him.
Well, Father, I have always found him just
The husband that I wished, and everything
That has pleased one of us has pleased the other.
I call that a good husband—but he's ruined,
You say; so now you mean to change me over
To one with property enough to save me
From all my troubles. Has he enough for that?
Where will you find such riches as can ever
Repay me for the man you take away?
And what of justice, what of decency,
If I who was full partner in his wealth
Am not allowed to share his poverty?

As for this man who means to marry me—
(Which God forbid, and which while I have will
And strength left in me, he shall never do!)
Suppose he, too, has losses, do you mean
To pass me on to a third? And if he fails,
To a fourth? How far do you intend to go,
Handing me round for your experiments

THE ARBITRATION

On Fortune? . . . Father, when I was a girl,
It was your business to decide what husband
To give me to. The choice was yours to make.
But once you've chosen and I have left your house—
My marriage is my own; and if I now
Judge wrongly it's my own life that I wreck.
Father, I beg you by our hearth and home,
Don't take me from this man into whose arms
You gave me. I ask simply what is fair
And kind. If you refuse, well, you'll have got
Your way by force, and I must try to bear
My lot without being utterly ashamed.

Smîcrinês
My child, I am saving you from certain ruin.

Pamphilê
"Saving"! But if your saving is a thing
You can't persuade me to, it's more a slave
You make me than a daughter.

Smîcrinês
                              My dear child,
Is it a case for arguing and persuading?
Isn't it obvious? Don't the facts themselves
Cry out? However, if you want me also
To argue, I'll just put a point or two.
First, child, your marriage is already wrecked,
Wrecked both for him and you. It's possible
He may enjoy himself, but certainly

77

THE ARBITRATION

You won't. You'd wish to be a loving wife?
You'll never be allowed. He doesn't want you.
If you persist in staying, do you mean him
To keep two houses? One for his new fancy
And one for you? He won't like the expense.
Everything doubled. All the household feasts,
Two Thesmophoria parties—very costly—
Two Skira feasts. Meantime, try to imagine
Your own life. Don't we know what it will be?
"Excuse him for to-day: urgent affairs
At the Piraeus." Off he goes, and doesn't
Come back, and you'll be hurt. You'll wait alone
Hour after hour, not dining till he comes;
You fasting while he's drinking with that girl!
God bless me, even now he has left the house
To join his harp-player. All right, I say;
You leave it too, for ever!

PAMPHILÊ

            May I speak?
I know Charisius. What I said about him
Just now is really true. He has never been
Unkind to me before. Something has changed him
In these last weeks. It may be I've displeased him
In some way I don't know. Some day he'll speak
About it and perhaps I can explain,
And be a better wife, and he'll forgive me . . .
At least, he may. And then he'll change again
And be himself. For me, I am quite content
To wait and hope. To go on as we are

THE ARBITRATION

At least a year or two will not use up
My dowry. I can live quite modestly.
And save on the housekeeping. I love my husband
And want to keep him.

SMÎCRINÊS

Can you hope to keep him?
Does *he* want to keep *you*? You have a rival.
More than a rival.

PAMPHILÊ

Only a dancing girl!
All young men have these fancies . . . though I never
Thought that *he* would; fancies that come and go;
Sudden, not lasting things. I am not afraid.

SMÎCRINÊS

It's not an equal battle, Pamphilê,
An honest woman matched against a whore:
They have the odds all round; they cheat and lie;
They have no shame; they flatter and deceive
In ways you never dream of; they know more;
They know the world, they know men's weaknesses . . .

PAMPHILÊ

I am more to him than a dozen dancing girls!

SMÎCRINÊS

Ah, but it's not a dozen. It's just one;
One only, and she the mother of his child.

THE ARBITRATION

He acknowledges the boy, accepts her word,
And next thing, I suppose, will set her free
And lodge her in this house. . . . You have no child.

PAMPHILÊ (*collapsing*)
Father, I'll go. This woman has more right
Than I have. She'll do better than I've done.
Send Sôphronê to help me, and I'll follow.

SMÎCRINÊS
Good, child; I knew that you'd be reasonable.
I'll fetch her; an old Nurse can give the sort
Of comfort that you need.

PAMPHILÊ (*embarrassed*)
                    Leave special orders
That she is to be admitted.

SMÎCRINÊS
                    Special orders?

PAMPHILÊ
I mean, the porter might not understand.
He might not let her in.

SMÎCRINES
                    Not let her in?
Bless me, I never heard such impudence.
I'll bring her here myself. I'll let them see
You have a father and a home and friends.
                              [*Exit* SMÎCRINÊS.

80

THE ARBITRATION

PAMPHILÊ

Friends, have I? Is there one that I can trust?
No one but Sôphronê; and there's no comfort
In her. If only she had had the courage
To help me at the first to tell Charisius!
But no; she said it was a thing all men
Are merciless about. It hurts their pride
Somehow. . . . Why can't they leave it to the Goddess?
Our sin is against her, not against them.
One might have thought that, if he knew, he'd feel
Pity, as I should for another girl
So battered. . . . But of course I don't know how
A man would feel, and Sôphronê was sure.
"Hide everything," she said; "Hide everything.
Hide most of all the child, and never dream
Of seeing him again. It's the only way
To save his life." Oh, I've grown almost blind
With weeping. . . . If I only had a mother
Or sister; I could tell my sister best.
She would have understood. But now . . . no sister
No child, no husband, none that I dare speak to . . .
And Artemis, they say, never forgives.

> [*She sits, forward L, pondering. Enter* HABRO-
> TONON *from House R., carrying the baby,
> wrapped in a torn crimson silk shawl. The
> two women do not see each other.*

HABROTONON

I'll take him with me and search—What, whimpering,
    is he?

THE ARBITRATION

Poor mite! I've no idea what's wrong with him.
> [*Sits, back near House.*

PAMPHILÊ
Is there no merciful god to pity me?

HABROTONON
Dear pretty, never mind! We'll find your mother;
We'll search the city for her.

PAMPHILÊ (*rising*)
Well, I'll go.
> [*She moves slowly towards the House;* HABROTONON
> *sees her for the first time, and stares.*

HABROTONON (*rising*)
Lady! One moment!

PAMPHILÊ
Did you call me?

HABROTONON
> Yes.

Please look at me, and see if you remember
Something.
> (PAMPHILÊ *gazes at her.*)
> It is! It's she! Oh, I'm so glad.

PAMPHILÊ
Who are you? What do you mean?

THE ARBITRATION

HABROTONON

                            Give me your hand.
Poor darling; tell me, did you go last year
To see the Tauropolia in a red
Tarentine silk?

PAMPHILÊ (*her eyes on the baby's shawl*)
                   Woman, where did you get
That baby?

HABROTONON
Do you recognize the shawl?
My dear . . . My dear, don't be afraid of me!

PAMPHILÊ
That's not your own child?

HABROTONON
                      No; I've passed it off
As mine . . . oh, not to do his mother wrong,
But to get time to find her. And I have!
I've found you! You're the girl I saw that night!

PAMPHILÊ (*bursts into tears, then grasping her*)
The man! Who was that man?

HABROTONON
                    Charisius.

PAMPHILÊ
                            No! . . .
Oh, bless you! Do you know it? Are you sure?

THE ARBITRATION

HABROTONON

Certain. But you: you came out of his house.
Aren't you his wife?

PAMPHILÊ

Yes.

HABROTONON

Happy, happy woman!
Some merciful god has pitied both of you.

[*Knocks are heard on the door of House L.*

Stop! Someone next door knocking! Take me in.
Here! To this house. I'll tell you everything.

[*Exeunt into House R.*
[*Enter* ONÊSIMUS *from House L.*

ONÊSIMUS

He's dotty! Upon my word he's going mad!
He *is* mad! No, but really, by the Gods,
He's off his head, Charisius, I mean,
My master. It's a cardiac paroxysm
Of the Black Gall, or something. I don't see
How else you can explain it. There he stood
Just now, ever so long, against the door,
Peering and listening, while just outside
Old Smîcrinês was grumbling to his daughter
All, I suppose, about this mess of ours.
As men of the world, I hardly like to tell you
How he kept changing colour: "O my sweetest,"
He cried. "What things you say!" and beat his head—
His own head! Then again, after a bit,

84

THE ARBITRATION

"God help me, what a wife I have had and lost!"
Then, when he'd heard all that there was to hear,
And crept away at last to his own room,
What groans and tearing of the hair! Just one
Continuous raving! "Blackguard that I am,"
He kept on, "when I had done a thing like that,
And made myself the father of a bastard,
To feel no pity, show no spark of mercy
To her in just the same plight! Barbarous!
Utterly heartless!" He's in such a state,
Half-mad, cursing himself and looking murder,
It's dangerous. I am all shrivelled up with fear.
As he is now, if he caught sight of me,
Who first obliged him with the information
About that baby, he might kill me dead.
No one has seen me slip out of the house,
But where to go to now, or what to think . . .
Ah! Someone coming out! I'm lost, I'm done for!
O Zeus the Saviour, save me if you can!

> [*Hides in the branches of the tree R.*
>
> [*Enter* CHARISIUS.

CHARISIUS

Am I a paragon? Always with an eye
For how things look! Such a discerning judge
Of honour and dishonour! So correct
And irreproachable in private life!
Some Power above has given me just the medicine
I needed, just the right appropriate thing
To make me see my vileness! "What," it says,
You miserable creature, puffed with pride

85

THE ARBITRATION

And fine words, so you can't forgive your wife
For—what? For being wronged, not doing wrong.
I'll make you see yourself in the same mess,
Blundering. I'll show you her all love and kindness
To you, and you all angry pride to her.
That ought to teach you what you are: pig-headed,
Hard-hearted, and most wretched all at once.
You heard her with her father? How like you!
"I am the partner of his life," she said:
"I cannot run away from the misfortune
"That's fallen upon him." Now, my high and mighty
Barbarian, what do you mean to do with her? . . .
Go, clasp her to your heart; beg her forgiveness!
Or may all Furies . . .! H'm. Of course there'll be
Her father too. He's sure to be hot-headed
And violent when he knows. Oh, damn her father!
I'll tell him bluntly: "My good Smîcrinês,
Let me alone. My wife's not leaving me.
Why make these storms and bully Pamphilê? . . ."

> [ONÊSIMUS, *peering round, falls out of tree with
> a crash.*

What? You again? What are you doing here?

ONÊSIMUS

Oh, this is quite bad; very bad. Ye Gods
Above me, help! Don't leave me in this soup!

CHARISIUS

You dirty dog, have you been skulking here
And listening?

THE ARBITRATION

Onêsimus

No; I swear.   I've just come out
This moment.

Charisius

Is there nothing one can keep
From you? I catch you hiding everywhere,
Onêsimus, listening to every word. . . .

Onêsimus

Isn't it natural I should try to hide
When you go round, like murder and damnation?

Charisius

Here, rogue, I'll teach you to know everything.
     [Onêsimus *runs away;* Charisius *pursues him.*
       [*Enter from the House* Habrotonon.

Habrotonon

Stop! Or you'll show that you yourself know nothing.

Charisius

Who's this? You?—What have you to do with this?
Why aren't you in the house, minding that baby?

Habrotonon

I have given it to its mother. It's not mine.

Charisius

Not yours? Not?—How? Was that whole tale a fraud
Of you two knaves?—Keep off, I'll see you later.

87

THE ARBITRATION

HABROTONON

Which will you do, send me away, or listen
To what we have to say, and learn the truth?

CHARISIUS

The truth . . . from two false disobedient slaves?

HABROTONON

Yes, hidden truth by a slave's trick revealed.

ONÊSIMUS

I was so frightened, Master. I just wanted
To experiment on you, to find you out . . .

CHARISIUS

To find me out . . . to experiment on me?

ONÊSIMUS

The woman made me. I take my oath she did.
                    [*Clasps* CHARISIUS'S *knees*.

CHARISIUS

Don't pull me about, you rogue!

HABROTONON

                        Don't beat the man!
Listen! It's great news. Listen!—Your own wife,
No poor strange girl, is mother to that child.

THE ARBITRATION

CHARISIUS

I wish to God it could be so.

HABROTONON

It is.
So may Demeter love me!

CHARISIUS

Fairy tales.
You're telling me!

HABROTONON

A fairy tale come true!

CHARISIUS

That boy is Pamphilê's? An hour ago
You told me it was mine.

HABROTONON

Yes. So it is.

CHARISIUS

And Pamphilê's? Habro, I'm serious.
Don't wing me with false hopes.

HABROTONON

The wings will bear you.
I told you I was at the Tauropolia
Last year, and that I saw—all that was true—
A girl alone, who ran out of the darkness
Weeping and terrified . . .

THE ARBITRATION

CHARISIUS
        Brute that I was!

HABROTONON
I did not know her name, but I remembered
Her face.

CHARISIUS
        You ought to have told me this before!

HABROTONON
How could I tell you till I knew myself?

CHARISIUS
Yes, I see that.

HABROTONON
        I had no clue, no guess,
Who the girl was, till now at your own door
I have seen her.

        CHARISIUS, *deeply moved, sits silently thinking.*

ONÊSIMUS
        There! I told you long ago
She'd had a baby . . .

HABROTONON
        Stupid! Hold your tongue!

THE ARBITRATION

CHARISIUS (*rising*)
The wrong I did was greater than I knew.
I'll ask her to forgive me. I'll go now.
[*Turning on his way to the House.*
I owe you a great debt. I promised you,
Freedom, Habrotonon, when I believed
You the child's mother. Well, that promise holds.

ONÊSIMUS
What about me? I found the ring. I started
The whole affair.

CHARISIUS
You rascal! All the mischief
You've made . . .

HABROTONON
must be forgiven, Master, now.
Without him I should never have unravelled
The secret; you would never have won back
Your wife and child. Rogue as he is, to you
He has been always faithful.

CHARISIUS
Yes; he's been
True to his master. . . . Well, I'll trust you still.
[*Exit into House A.*

91

THE ARBITRATION

HABROTONON (*to herself, deeply moved*)
Freedom! O Saviour Gods, I bless your name!

ONÊSIMUS (*jubilant*)
I knew I'd pull it off. I always do.

ACT V

Enter SÎMIAS *and* CHAERESTRATUS *talking.*

SÎMIAS

We mustn't seem to avoid a friend in trouble.
The child is his. He gave the girl his word
For that before a dozen witnesses.
There's no way out. Well, you must just remain
A good friend to Charisius—Good, remember,
And true! That girl is not a common slave;
In heart and character she's a free woman.
Besides, she's now the mother of his child.
Therefore, Halt! No more ogling of the harpist!

CHAERESTRATUS

Why should you think I need all this advice?
I've no desire to ogle anyone,
Nor offer anyone condolences,
Nor yet congratulations. I'd just sooner
Be left alone. You go to him.

SÎMIAS

        All right.
I'll do my best to find some words of comfort
For poor Charisius and his bonny boy!
Well, here goes! (*seeing* HABROTONON) Prudence,
    prudence!

    [*As he goes into the House,* HABROTONON *enters
       and is going towards the House when* CHAE-
       RESTRATUS *speaks.*

THE ARBITRATION

CHAERESTRATUS (*stiffly*)
>> Pray allow me,
To offer you my warm congratulations.
I hear you are promised freedom.

HABROTONON
>> Thank you, Sir,
That is so.

CHAERESTRATUS
And perhaps still further honours?

HABROTONON
What higher honour is there?

CHAERESTRATUS
>> Marriage?

HABROTONON
>> No;
I have not heard of any.

CHAERESTRATUS
>> But that child . . .

HABROTONON
Is with his mother. I'm just going to her.

CHAERESTRATUS
His mother?

THE ARBITRATION

HABROTONON

Pamphilê.

CHAERESTRATUS (*amazed*)
Has Pamphilê
Bought it, or what? You said the child was yours.

HABROTONON

I had my reasons.

CHAERESTRATUS
Then that rigmarole
You told . . .

HABROTONON
Has served its purpose. Now we know
Not all of it was true.

CHAERESTRATUS
A lie to make him
Believe the child was yours!

HABROTONON
Yes. Slaves are good
At lying. It's our chief accomplishment.

CHAERESTRATUS
You did him a great wrong! Made him confess
The child was his!

THE ARBITRATION

HABROTONON

It was. The ring proved that.
And when I once knew that, I had the clue
To find its mother.

CHAERESTRATUS

But why should you find her?
If she was found you lost all claim upon him.
You were no more the mother of his child;
Why should he set you free?

HABROTONON

I took that risk.

CHAERESTRATUS

That risk! The risk of being held a slave
For ever!

HABROTONON

What a slave I should have been,
And worse, if I had tried to hide the truth?

CHAERESTRATUS

I never knew a slave before who felt
In that way.

HABROTONON

Why, what else was there to do?
Slave as I am, and hungering to be free,
I have a woman's heart. How could I leave
That child cast out and helpless, a free child

96

THE ARBITRATION

Born of a gentle house? Or how could I
Forget that wronged girl at the midnight feast?
Great liars as we slaves are, we can be honest.

CHAERESTRATUS

You had your freedom safe, and took the risk
Of losing it again!

HABROTONON
        Safe, would you say?
No; any chance might have upset my story
And covered me with shame.
            [*Enter* MAID *from House R. with tray.*
                Are those the tokens?
You're taking them to the mistress? Leave them here.
I'll take them (*exit* MAID). Think how deadly these
        would be
Against me! Look, except Charisius' ring,
They are all her things, not mine (*looking through them*).
                I never wore
Gold chains and precious stones . . . though once I had
A silver cup like that . . . rather like that.

CHAERESTRATUS

You, as a child?

HABROTONON
        Oh, I was quite a baby.
It had my name engraved, like Pamphilê's
On this.

THE ARBITRATION

CHAERESTRATUS
It looks as if there'd been some name
Cut out here; and then Pamphilê's inscribed
Above it.

HABROTONON
Oh, of course the cup is hers!
I never meant to claim it. I don't even
Remember properly what mine was like.

CHAERESTRATUS (*looking at the cup*)
There was some name; but not Habrotonon.

HABROTONON
Habrotonon! Who'd give a child a name
Like that, a poor hired slave-performer's name,
Like "Pegs-and-strings" or "Catgut"? No; I had
A real name once.

CHAERESTRATUS
What was it?

HABROTONON
I don't know.
Some grown-up name. They never called me by it . . .
They called me . . . Oh, just silly baby names.

CHAERESTRATUS
What was your father's name?

98

THE ARBITRATION

HABROTONON

How should I know?
I called him Dadda. I was very little.

CHAERESTRATUS (*with the cup*)
A K I can make out, and perhaps an L;
Kle, Kleo—

HABROTONON

Kleo— No; I'm only guessing.
I half thought . . . That's enough! I can quite see
What you expect; you think I'm going to tell you
The usual slave's romance, how I was born
Quite free and rich, but captured in the wars
Or lost at sea. You won't believe a word!
Why should you? I've no shred of proof to back
My fables.

CHAERESTRATUS

I believe your every word.
I know you are free at heart, too true, too proud
For tricks that one can pardon in a slave.
But do try to remember. Any detail
Might give us clues . . .

HABROTONON

I haven't any clues!
I knew so little. I can just remember
Men fighting in the streets. I lost my doll.
And a man came and took me by the hand
And said: "Come on, my dear. The other children
Are waiting." So he took me to the Gate,

99

THE ARBITRATION

And there there was a crowd, and I was put
Among the smallest girls, and we were sold
Quickly, in bunches, to the slave-dealers.
Then later I was taught to play the harp
And given that stupid name . . . Oh, it's all useless.
I don't know where it was. I don't remember
My father's name. Most likely I never knew it.
I have no proofs.

CHAERESTRATUS

What need have I of proofs?
Charisius is your guardian? I propose
To-day to ask him his ward's hand in marriage.

HABROTONON

No, no! I need some time to think; to learn
How to be free; to sit and taste my freedom;
Lie on the ground and whisper to the Earth
"Free, Mother, free at last!" No more unclean,
No more a coward! I want to wash my body,
And clean my soul of slavish fears and stains;
And be no more, in my own thoughts, as yours,
That harp-girl who was hired to smile and play,
Be kissed and revel at some drunken feast,
Or else be beaten. I want time to breathe . . .
—I must take in these things to Pamphilê.

> [*She picks up the tray. Enter from House* SÎMIAS;
> *behind him* ONÊSIMUS, *a large drinking cup
> in his hands, watches with interest.* CHAERE-
> STRATUS *tries to hold* HABROTONON, *but she
> slips by into the House.*

THE ARBITRATION

CHAERESTRATUS

But listen. Stay a moment.

SÎMIAS

What's all this?
Chaerestratus, I warned you!

CHAERESTRATUS

Yes, you did!
You did! But wasn't that some time ago?
Hasn't there been a change?

SÎMIAS (*taken aback*)

Why, so there has.
I always said that girl ought to be free.
And if she's free . . . But you're so hasty. Come,
Let's talk it over.

[*Exeunt together to House B.*

ONÊSIMUS

There he goes again!
After the harping girl! Well, I don't mind.
That girl's too clever for me. I can never
Quite make her out . . . I must say she's played fair
About our partnership. I've got full pardon
For everything, and special thanks for finding
That baby. I've not got liberty, like her.
But, Lord, why should I want it? She'll go free,
And lodge alone and work and weave and sew,
Eat little, wear cheap clothes, and sometimes get

101

THE ARBITRATION

On her good days a chance to play that harp
At temples: no more banqueting for her!
I like a big house, plenty of good grub,
Plenty of people, lots of news and gossip,
And secrets to find out. Besides I'm now
A privileged and powerful person, I'm
Trusted with secrets! . . . She's a pretty baggage
No doubt. Chaerestratus is quite right there.
Ah, what it is to have a temperate
Abstemious mind! (*takes a long drink*) If he'd had half
    my chances,
I bet he never could have kept his hands
Off such a girl. I can, by Jove, and will.
Here comes . . . Hullo! I'll have a lark with him.

                               [*Exit.*

       [*Enter* SMÎCRINÊS *and* SÔPHRONÊ, *arguing.*

SMÎCRINÊS

That's what you think? Plague take me, Sôphronê,
If I don't break your head! You'll scold me too,
Like all the others? Hasty, am I? Hasty,
Claiming my daughter back, you god-forsaken
Old reptile? Do you want me to sit smiling
While her egregious husband wolfs up all
Her dowry? And just talk and talk in hopes
To save my property? You're like the rest . . .
No, sharp's the word! So no more talk from you.
I've no dispute with anyone except
My daughter. As for you, I brought you here
Simply to make my daughter change her mind,

THE ARBITRATION

And be obedient—quickly—Sôphronê,
On our way home . . . I think you saw that pond
In passing . . . in that pond I mean to duck you
All night until you choke, or may I never
Know happiness again! I only want you
To see I'm right and not keep picking quarrels.
H'm, I must knock. The blessèd door is barred.
Ho, boys, there! Porter! Someone hurry up
And open. Why the Devil can't they hear me?

        [*Enter* ONÊSIMUS (*still with the cup*).

ONÊSIMUS

Who's knocking at the door? Oh, Smîcrinês
The furious, come to fetch his precious dowry
And daughter!

SMÎCRINÊS

      Yes, you infernal jackanapes.

ONÊSIMUS

How right you are! One sees you have a brain
Both philosophic and executive,
Good for abduction, good for burglary;
Splendid, by Hercules!

SMÎCRINÊS

      O Gods and devils!

ONÊSIMUS

Gods? So you think the Gods have time to apportion

THE ARBITRATION

The appropriate bane and blessing, day by day,
To each man? . . . Do you really, Smîcrinês?

SMÎCRINÊS
What are you talking about?

ONÊSIMUS
Let me explain.
It's simple. There are cities in the world,
At least a hundred thousand. In each city
Say, thirty thousand citizens. The Gods,
You think, keep watch on each of these, all day
And every day, giving them all their due
Of good and evil?

SMÎCRINÊS
What's all this?

ONÊSIMUS
I think
That works the Gods too hard. "Then don't they care
For human kind at all?" Of course they do.
They've billeted on every citizen
A special guardian, called his Temperament.
He's our unsleeping watchman. Use him wrong,
He'll plague you; right, and he's your preservation.
(You've never read psychology? Of course not.)
Our Temperament, why it's the God who guides
Each one of us, the cause of all our troubles
And pleasures. If you wish for happiness
Implore this God not to go doing things
Absurd or inconsiderate.

104

THE ARBITRATION

SMÎCRINÊS

What, you rascal?
It's doing something inconsiderate now,
My temperament?

ONÊSIMUS

Your temperament's the plague
Of your whole life.

SMÎCRINÊS

Infernal impudence!

ONÊSIMUS

Well, really, do you think it a good thing
To abduct one's daughter from her husband? Really?

SMÎCRINÊS

Who says it's a good thing? It's only a thing
That must be done.

ONÊSIMUS

You see? The man maintains
A bad thing is a thing "that must be done."
Who sends him mad if not his Temperament?
However, it so happens that, before
You had time to do this bad thing, a pure chance
Has saved you. You've come just in time to find
Peace signed and those old troubles all washed out.
Let this be a lesson to you, Smîcrinês.
Don't let me ever catch you again behaving
So violently! Come in now; no more talk
Of grievances, and welcome to your arms
Your grandson.

THE ARBITRATION

SMÎCRINÊS

Grandson, you infernal rogue?

ONÊSIMUS (*laughing helplessly*)

You wooden-head, you thought you were so clever,
Like lots of other fathers! That's the way
You watch over a marriageable girl!
No wonder we've strange babies to bring up,
Miraculous five-monthers!

SMÎCRINÊS

I don't know
What you are talking about.

ONÊSIMUS

The old woman does,
Unless I am much mistaken . . . Sôphronê,
The Tauropolia; it was there my master
Found her alone; she had somehow lost the choir
She played in, and . . . you understand?

SÔPHRONÊ

Of course.

ONÊSIMUS

And now there's been a mutual recognition,
And all's well.

SMÎCRINÊS

What does he mean, you wicked woman?

THE ARBITRATION

SÔPHRONÊ

"So Nature willed, who, heeding not man's laws
Invented women for this very cause."

SMÎCRINÊS

Have you gone mad?

SÔPHRONÊ
Must I recite a whole
Tragic oration from Euripides?
I will if you can't see.

SMÎCRINÊS
It makes me sick,
Your tragic stuff. You see only too well
What this man means?

SÔPHRONÊ
Of course. I knew it all.

ONÊSIMUS

You bet your life. She knew it long ago,
That old nurse.

SMÎCRINÊS
I'm disgraced.

SÔPHRONÊ
Not you, unless
You choose to assume you are.

SMÎCRINÊS
It's terrible!

THE ARBITRATION

SÔPHRONÊ

There never was a grander stroke of luck,
If this man's story is true. Our baby's father . . .

ONÊSIMUS

Is certainly Charisius. He admits it.

SMÎCRINÊS

Is that the word? Of course it's his; and now
The scoundrel dares to claim that Pamphilê's
Its mother, so as not to lose my dowry.
He's welcome to his bastards. But my daughter
Is different. She has always been obedient,
And good. I don't believe a word of it.

SÔPHRONÊ

I know the child was hers.

SMÎCRINÊS

What reason have I
To trust your word?

SÔPHRONÊ

Ask Pamphilê herself.

SMÎCRINÊS

She loves that scoundrel. She'd say anything
To win him back to her. How do I know
You're not all in a plot to torture me
And save Charisius?

THE ARBITRATION

SÔPHRONÊ

Have you seen the tokens?

[*Calling to the House.*

Habrotonon, kindly bring those tokens out.

[HABROTONON *brings them on the tray.*

These were the things set out beside the baby
When he was found. I know: I put them there;
I kept close watch upon him all the time,
And these are what I took from Pamphilê.

SMÎCRINÊS (*examining them*)

They're not all hers. I never saw that ring.

SÔPHRONÊ

Charisius' ring, that is.

SMÎCRINÊS

This silver cup,
This wasn't Pamphilê's.

HABROTONON

Not hers? I wonder
Can it be really mine?

SMÎCRINÊS

Yours? This cup yours?
This was my elder daughter's cup.

THE ARBITRATION

HABROTONON

I am sorry.
I thought it looked like . . . May I look again?
[SMÎCRINÊS *snatches it up.*
I know mine had my name engraved inside it.

SMÎCRINÊS

What name?

HABROTONON

I don't know. I was very little.
Some grown-up name. They never called me by it.

SMÎCRINÊS

You don't know your own name. Perhaps you know
Your mother's name?

HABROTONON

We only called her Mother.

SMÎCRINÊS

Where did your father live?

HABROTONON

It was some island,
I think.

SMÎCRINÊS

Some island: which? (HABROTONON *is silent*)
I never heard
A feebler piece of fraud. I should have thought
In your profession you'd acquire more skill.

THE ARBITRATION

HABROTONON

No, it's no good. It was a baby world
I lived in.

SMÎCRINÊS

That's enough. Back to your quarters!
One bastard grandchild's quite enough for me,
Without a harping slave-girl for a daughter.

[HABROTONON *turns away, discomfited.* SÔPHRONÊ
has been looking closely at her.

SÔPHRONÊ

Grasshopper!

HABROTONON (*turning suddenly*)
Grasshopper! Who calls me that?
Who is it? . . . Sôpho! No! You can't be Sôpho.

SÔPHRONÊ (*embraces* HABROTONON)
Grasshopper darling!

SMÎCRINÊS

Stop! We have no proof!

SÔPHRONÊ

Be quiet, you stupid man! Haven't you said
Enough of harsh things you'll be sorry for?

ONÊSIMUS

Great Gods! Chaerestratus must know of this!

[*Exit to House B.*

111

THE ARBITRATION

SÔPHRONÊ

What happened, child, the day we lost you? Can you
Remember anything?

HABROTONON
A little. I
Was with my mother.

SÔPHRONÊ
On the temple steps.
I left you while we tried to find a boat.

HABROTONON
Then suddenly she was gone. I couldn't find her.

SMÎCRINÊS
I found her.

HABROTONON
Yes; and then a man came up
Smiling and said, "Come, dear; the other children
Are waiting."

SÔPHRONÊ
So you went with him?

HABROTONON
Why, yes.

SMÎCRINÊS
Why did you go with him?

THE ARBITRATION

HABROTONON

          He took my hand.
Besides, he sounded kind. Only I lost
My doll.

SMÎCRINÊS

I know. I found it by her body.

HABROTONON

And so he brought us to the slave-dealers
Down by the quay, and sold us.

SMÎCRINÊS

          Oh, my child!
Forgive me. I have wronged you. I am old
And bitter, and see all things through a blur
Of loss and anger and bewilderment.
So many evil things I have seen and suffered.
By wars and wicked men: all whom I loved
Lost but one daughter, whom I sought to save
Too harshly, from dishonour—Sôphronê,
Take this great news to Pamphilê.

      [SÔPHRONÊ *and* HABROTONON *go in together.*

          Great wrongs
They have suffered, both, but who dares speak the word
Dishonour? Both I count as innocent
And honourable women.

      [*Re-enter* SÔPHRONÊ, *with* HABROTONON, PAM-
        PHILÊ *and* CHARISIUS. PAMPHILÊ *carrying*
        the Baby.

THE ARBITRATION

Clearista,
You shall be free by nightfall. I shall pay
Your price this afternoon.

CHARISIUS

Excuse me, Sir,
This lady has done me a service past all counting,
And I have promised faithfully myself
To pay her ransom.

[*Enter* CHAERESTRATUS *with* ONÊSIMUS.

SÔPHRONÊ

Well, be quick about it.
Whoever it is. Her owners mustn't hear
This story, or they'll raise her price beyond
Your worst foreboding.

CHAERESTRATUS

Quite the contrary.
Leave this to me. I have some little knowledge
Of the Attic courts. I'll call upon these rascals
And face them with the charge that "by mere fraud
And violence they detain in slavery
A f.ee-born body." They'll give in at once.
They must.

SMÎCRINÊS

What a remarkable young man!
Such knowledge of the law and such good sense
Combined! (*to* CHARISIUS) My son-in-law, this man
    speaks well;
Who is he?

THE ARBITRATION

CHAERESTRATUS
Sir, your second son-in-law,
With your permission!   [*Takes* HABROTONON'S *arm.*

SMÎCRINÊS
This is all too much
For me to understand. Yes; I'm bewildered.
Clearista, what say you?

HABROTONON
Well, this time Yes.
I am dreaming: how can I refuse a dream?
Is this still you and I? So changed we seem
And moved to a new world. Can this be me
And yonder Sôpho and here Pamphilê,
And father? A new world!

PAMPHILÊ
And where will you
Place him to whom the world is really new,
The man new-born, a symbol of that breath
Each year by which the race is snatched from death?
He has no past: his morning sweeps away
All clouds.
SMÎCRINÊS
Nay, child, there is a yesterday
Always. Past evil leaves a stress of dread
Under all joy. Have not our sages said,
When wounded men, lulled to oblivion deep
By that Egyptian poppy, slowly creep

THE ARBITRATION

Toward sense again, the first thing that they know
Is pain, for pain is life? Each infant so
By his first wailing makes good prophecy,
For man 'tis pain to live and pain to die.

SÔPHRONÊ

Pain first, but after . . . wonder, longing, strife,
Adventure, hopes and fears; all these are life;
Defeat, success, the worship of some truth
Or phantom, all the battle-joys of youth,
And ways of thought that, as youth fades, may still
Fill age with fragrance. Man, for good or ill,
And all his race, is even as this child
I saved, a frail thing, homeless in the wild,
Part pain, part hope, all daring; and who knows
Whence here it came or whither hence it goes?
For this the Man-Babe lives, these things to do
And suffer; thus he makes the world anew
At each new birth, still facing to a day
Unknown, and still the hero of his play.

NOTES

THE scene is an open space with two Houses at the back, as usual in the New Comedy. The tree makes it easier for two people to be on the stage together without seeing each other—a situation which often occurs.

The conceited and pedantic Cook is a regular New Comedy character, and so is the valet or personal attendant, a cunning rogue, stupid and not over-honest, but genuinely devoted to his young master.

As to the names, they come from the stock of New Comedy. As in Restoration Comedy, they have meanings more or less suitable to the character; Pamphilê, "*All-dear*"; Onêsimus, "*Helpful*"; Sôphronê, "*Prudence.*" Habrotonon, meaning something like "*softly or delicately tuned,*" is a name suited to a harpist's profession. The two slave names Syriscus and Dâvus mean respectively, "*Little Syrian*" and "*Davian,*" the Davi being a nomad tribe in Asia. Charisius has a suggestion of "Pleasantness," Smîcrinês a suggestion of "meanness." The names, however, are all real names taken from ordinary life; they are not artificial inventions like "Lady Wishfor't," "Sir John Brute," or "Sneerwell," in English comedy.

THE ARBITRATION

ACT I

p. 14. Sôphronê, as we shall see in Act V, is a silent person who gets her way. She has more brains and more experience than the others.

p. 19. Chaerestratus is not a "young puppy," but an interesting character. He is torn between his obvious, though unspoken, love for Habrotonon, and his dislike of getting mixed up in a rowdy party or a dishonourable intrigue.

p. 23. Small coins were usually carried in the mouth or the hand. (See Blaydes on Aristophanes, *Eccles*. 818.) For bulkier things a fold of the gown could be girded up as a pocket.

p. 24. PROLOGUE.—Menander's Prologues seem generally to have come in this position, as second scenes after a first scene meant to rouse curiosity and require explanation. In parody of the tragic prologue, they are generally spoken by non-human characters with a touch of the absurd about them, like the goddess Ignorance in the *Rape of the Locks*. Callisto's account of herself here is roughly in agreement with the story told by Hygînus and others, though no one seems to have mentioned the "fourteen years' hard labour." Elsewhere she either remained a bear or became a constellation.

p. 26. "all murderous males." By ancient law the father had an absolute right to decide whether the child

NOTES

presented to him should or should not be reared. If it proved to be the illegitimate child of his wife its chances would be small.

p. 27. Smîcrinês (from *smikros*, "small") is said to have been a name used in Comedy for misers. This Smîcrinês has some miserly traits but is in general like one of the regular "cross old men." He becomes progressively humanized as the play proceeds.

p. 28. Four talents, in gold about £960, was quite a large dowry for the time. Polemo in the *Locks* was pleased with three. The purchasing power of money was vastly greater than now, and 10 per cent. a usual rate of interest. Two obols a day was the regular "dole" for a pauper. See Tarn in *The Hellenistic Age* (Cambridge, 1932).

p. 29. "Some pessimist philosopher." Philosophy was, for various reasons, a matter of great general interest at the time. Menander is said to have been a close friend of Epicurus.

p. 32. "Young lads, and not too sober." This is the cue for the entry of a Chorus of professional Dancers, performing a sort of ballet as an *entr'acte*. The Chorus in the New Comedy had ceased to be an integral part of the play. The song supplied here is based on a famous lyric in the style of Anacreon. The youths are garlanded and wild but not tipsy. They may be so when the revel breaks up in Act III.

THE ARBITRATION

ACT II

p. 34. These soliloquies, intended partly to reveal character, partly just to keep the audience informed, however unrealistic they seem to us, were a favourite device of Menander's, and show one side of his art.

p. 34. Young Habro: I venture, in accordance with a common Greek custom, to shorten Habrotonon's name.

pp. 38–53. This scene, which has given the play its name, is fortunately preserved in full on the papyrus, together with the rest of the Act. Dâvus is a rough rustic; Syriscus a more brainy and polished oriental; but both are poor slaves in goatskin cloaks.

p. 45. Nêleus and Pelias: Both were heroes of tragedies of the Nativity Play type. To our taste this speech is obviously too long. To the original audience there was amusement in the references to tragedy and also in the surprising rhetorical fluency of the charcoal-burner.

p. 49. "After the rents are paid." Apparently Syriscus and Dâvus were tenants of Charisius and had come up for a rent-day.

p. 52. "His friend next door. . . . The same house." Did the two neighbouring villas have their slave-quarters in common?

120

NOTES

ACT III

p. 54. Note how Onêsimus is constantly shifting from one extreme to another, from over-confidence to terror, from belief in his own cleverness to suspicion that he has made a fool of himself. See, for example, his changes on pp. 65 and 84, or the last words in Act IV, p. 92.

It is in this Act that Habrotonon's character first becomes visible. She is a free-born and courageous girl, now a slave. She has learned enough of the impudence and cynicism of her trade, to be able to use them when necessary, but essentially her feelings towards the exposed baby, the wronged girl and the tipsy and ill-mannered young man, are those of a free woman, womanly, self-respecting, and generous. Menander treats with a curious reticence the tragedy which forms the background of Habrotonon. It is indicated by a phrase or two, like "I know it well enough" on p. 61, and the mention of her innocence at the time of last year's Tauropolia, but does not come out clearly, if I read the author's intention right, till the end of the play. The real slave, Onêsimus, is incapable of understanding her.

p. 54. Habrotonon apparently came away at some early stage of the dinner, and returned to the company during dessert, though, owing to Cârion's inordinate delays dessert had not yet been reached.

"Free from contact": in the strict sense. He had not even shaken hands with her.

THE ARBITRATION

p. 56. Tauropolia. This is the first mention of a feast called Tauropolia in Attica. It seems to refer to the festival of Artemos Tauropolos at Brauron, in which we happen to know that there was a dance or performance of young girls—over the age of ten—pretending to be bears.

p. 57. "That this charcoal-burner found." Habrotonon did not know it was the shepherd who really found the baby.

p. 59. Tarentine. A "Tarentine" was a light, almost diaphanous wrap made of the byssus, or fine linen of South Italy. The word is also applied to silk.

p. 61. "I know it well enough." Evidently Habrotonon's owners had not made her go out as a *hetaira* to banquets until quite lately. This fits in with the intensity of her feelings about the unknown girl at the Tauropolia and about slavery in Act V.

p. 72. Daric. A Persian gold coin with a head of Darius.

ACT IV

pp. 75 ff. A curious critical question arises about the opening of this Act. There is a gap in our text of about 23 lines in one place and about 94 later, just before Habrotonon's entrance. It must have contained Smîcrinês's scene with his daughter, persuading her to leave her husband. Now it so happens that on a papyrus published by Weil in 1879 there is a speech of

NOTES

44 lines in which a young wife pleads with her father not to make her leave her husband. It is headed in the papyrus "Euripides," and seems to have been set as a school exercise. It is certainly not Euripides, and almost certainly came from some play of the New Comedy. Professor D. S. Robertson has made the very attractive suggestion that it comes from this play and this place. The fit is not perfect; but the situation is extremely similar; and the line of pleading is just what Pamphilê might well have used. Her speech gives a fine picture of a loving and dutiful wife, according to the ideas of Menandrian Athens, but of course one must also remember her secret. She knows that there is an excuse for Charisius which must not be mentioned.

p. 78. The Thesmophoria and Skira were two of the great Athenian festivals. It seems curious that they should bulk so large in the supposed expenses of Charisius, but that is characteristic of ancient Greek life, or indeed that of any simple society; a very frugal daily life with great outbursts on the important festivals.

pp. 82 ff. This recognition scene must be taken slowly and involves a good deal of silent acting. It is a characteristic of Menander's style to alternate scenes in which the language is everything with others in which little is said and much indicated.

p. 84. "As men of the world." Onêsimus frankly addresses the audience. This deliberate breach of the illusion is a trick that has lasted on from Aristophanes to modern farce.

THE ARBITRATION

p. 84. In the stage convention doors usually opened outwards. You knocked to warn people in the street.

p. 85. The bitter self-reproach of Charisius is interesting and shows the vast gulf between the moral ideas of Menander and those of Wycherley or Congreve. He is ashamed of his own action; at the same time it makes him understand his wife's. She had been carried away by the excitements of the Midnight Revel, as he was, and also was far less a free agent.

pp. 87 ff. Habrotonon speaks with calm, almost with authority; Charisius is angry and bewildered; Onêsimus utterly frightened.

ACT V

p. 98. "Pegs-and-strings or Catgut." See p. 117. "Habrotonon" was a name denoting her profession as a slave musician. Her real name, we find, was Clearista.

p. 100. The slave dealers. They would naturally gather round a besieged or sacked town to buy up prisoners of war or children whose parents were lost or could not take care of them. Xenophon tells how Agêsilaus, King of Sparta, made arrangements for protecting such children and old people when he took a town (*Ages.* I. 21).

p. 100. A free woman would normally have a "guardian" of some sort, to be responsible for her

NOTES

before the law. As Habrotonon had no husband or older male relation it seems that Charisius, if he had bought her and set her free, would act.

p. 101. "work and weave and sew." The virtuous free woman without a family was apt to have a hard life, as we see from Terence.

pp. 103 ff. Onêsimus, presumably under the influence of his wine, proceeds to talk philosophy. Philosophers were a strong influence in Athens at the time.

p. 111. "Grasshopper." The Greek name of the cicada, "Tettix," was sometimes given to children. We even hear of men so called.

GEORGE ALLEN & UNWIN LTD
LONDON: 40 MUSEUM STREET, W.C.1
CAPE TOWN: 58–60 LONG STREET
TORONTO: 91 WELLINGTON STREET WEST
BOMBAY: 15 GRAHAM ROAD, BALLARD ESTATE
WELLINGTON, N.Z.: 8 KINGS CRESCENT, LOWER HUTT
SYDNEY, N.S.W.: BRADBURY HOUSE, 55 YORK STREET